Cram Course
for the
SAT*

Cram Course for the

SAT

Ronald G. Vlk

ARCO
New York

ARCO

Simon & Schuster, Inc.
Gulf+Western Building
One Gulf+Western Plaza
New York, NY 10023

DISTRIBUTED BY PRENTICE HALL TRADE

Designed by Harold Chester
Manufactured in the United States of America

3 4 5 6 7 8 9 10

Library of Congress Cataloging-in-Publication Data

Vlk, Ronald G.
  Cram Course for the SAT

  1. Scholastic aptitude test—Study guides. I. Title.
LB2353.57.V55 1985   378'.1662   85-11081
ISBN 0-13-188707-6 (Paper Edition)

CONTENTS

PREFACE

Why Use the 10-hour Plan?

There are many people who cannot or simply will not spend more than 10 hours studying for an exam. If you agree with one or more of the following statements, this book is just right for you.

1. I am not certain whether or not I am actually going to take the SAT; I just want a book that I can browse through to determine what types of questions are on the exam and how hard they will be.

2. I haven't decided whether to take the SAT and go to college, take the ACT and go to a private school, or just take a vocational exam and go to technical school. I want some books that are short enough to enable me to go through more than one to help me make my choice.

3. I know I will be taking the SAT sometime, but I don't know when. I want a short book I can skim through to help me determine whether I will need to take any special courses (such as more math) to prepare myself for taking the exam a few years down the road.

4. I am the type who needs discipline and has trouble working without a specific study plan. This 10-hour format, with everything organized for me, will help me stick to my studies and not quit halfway through.

5. I don't have a lot of money and really don't want to gamble the cost of a full-length test preparation book; however, I won't miss the few dollars spent on this book (even if for some reason I decide not to take the exam).

6. I am in school and have studies and social activities that take up much of my time. I want a short book that I can work through,

not a long intimidating tome that will take more time than I can or will give.

7.   I suddenly decided to take the SAT and was dismayed to find out that the exam is being given in just a few weeks/days. I don't have time to go through a lengthy study program; 10 hours sounds just right.

8.   I have already taken the SAT (or other exams somewhat similar to it) and don't think I need to do a great deal of studying again. All I need is a brief review that will tell me what similarities and differences this exam has from the other exam(s) I took.

9.   I have already taken an SAT preparation course (at school or through a private test preparation business). I feel I am prepared, but I want some sort of quick refresher.

10.   I just found out that test preparation books exist; I want to gain the maximum benefits from studying but only have a short time to do so.

Do any of the above statements sound familiar? Perhaps you found yourself making them to your family or friends, or muttering them to yourself as you stood in front of the many test preparation books displayed in a bookstore. This book is written for you, the person who wants to do the job quickly but well. To find out how to minimize the pain and maximize the gain, turn to the introduction where you will find the 10-hour plan explained in detail.

1.

DAY ONE

Hour One: Introduction to the 10-hour Concept

Set Your Clock. You were promised a 10-hour study plan; a 10-hour study plan is what you will get. Your 10 hours begin now with your reading of this Introduction and your working through the exercises given herein. The Introduction should take you just under an hour; the second hour of your first two-hour block of time will be spent on the section entitled "The SAT."

This book has been very carefully designed to give you all the information you need in a concise format so that you can do an excellent job of studying for the SAT in just 10 hours. These 10 hours are to be broken up into five 2-hour sessions. NOTE: It is strongly suggested that you do indeed study in units of two hours at a time; however, some units are written so that you can break them up into 1-hour segments. For example, on Day One you could read this Introduction and work through the exercises in one hour. You could, if absolutely necessary, do the second hour's worth of work on another day. The same thing applies with Day Two; if you absolutely had to, you could spend just one hour on the first segment (antonyms and analogies), then come back to the second hour (sentence completion and reading comprehension) another day.

Exercise One: Setting Up Your Schedule

At the end of this book you will find a "calendar." As you can see, the calendar is a study organizer, a chart telling you what you will be studying on which day and for how long. This is only a suggested organization. You may, if you wish, change the order of the sections, with one exception. You *must* do Day One's material (that is, this Introduction and the section entitled "The SAT") on the first day. If you do not do so, you will be completely confused by subsequent instructions and information.

Take the time right now to fill in on your calendar exactly which days and which hours you will use to study. If at all possible, try to set aside the same hours every day. You may wish to study before school (or work), from 6:00 to 8:00 A.M. daily. You may prefer to study in the evenings, from 7:00 to 9:00 P.M. Whatever hours you choose, do try to use two hours in a row, at a time when you will not be disturbed by others. Using the same hours daily will help you stick to your schedule.

The following are some factors you should consider when planning your study schedule:

1.   What hours may I set aside without feeling guilty for neglecting my regular school studies?

2.   What hours may I set aside where I will not be disturbed (by parents, friends, or siblings)?

3.   Will I be able to stick to those hours, even if they fall on a weekend or a holiday?

4.   Am I fresh enough to study during those hours? (You may not want to study from 10:00 P.M. to midnight, after you are exhausted from a long day.)

5.   Are my hours of study realistic? (Many persons swear to themselves that they will actually get up at 4:00 A.M. to study; such good intentions usually last one day at most!)

All right, you have now filled in your study schedule and are determined to stick to it. However, there probably will be some variations; how you deal with them will significantly affect your overall success on this study program.

Missing a Day. What happens if you become ill, or you have an obligation elsewhere, and cannot study on a particular day? First of all, don't become overly concerned. Do not automatically assume that your study plan is ruined and that you may as well give up the whole thing. There are several alternatives you should consider.

1. *Make up the lost time on the same day.* If at all possible, the best way to make up the time is to set aside two hours (or at least one) on that *same day*. Even if you have to give up your favorite television program or your evening aerobics class, try to fit in your studying on that very day. Not only will you stick to your schedule somewhat, you will feel wonderfully virtuous.

2. *Make up the lost time by doubling up your study time on another day.* This means that instead of studying two hours on another day, you study four hours that day. While this is not recommended, you may find that it is your only option. If you must put in four hours on one day, break them up as much as possible. Try to put in two hours in the morning and two in the evening. At the very least, take a half-hour break between the sessions; get up and walk around.

3. *Make up the lost time by adding another day on the end of your study schedule.* Of course, this is the optimum alternative; simply study Monday through Saturday instead of Monday through Friday. However, you may find that your schedule is too tight to allow you to do this.

4. *Skip a section entirely.* This is the last thing you want to do, but you may find it is your only alternative. If you absolutely cannot add another day to your study schedule, and you cannot study more than two hours a day, your only choice is to skip one day's worth of study. If that is your plan, by all means be careful to skip that day from which you would gain the least. You will have to make a personal decision whether you can best afford to neglect a verbal section (antonyms, analogies, sentence completion, or reading comprehension), a mathematical section (quantitative comparison or problem solving), or a grammar section (usage or sentence correction).

What you do not want to do is to skim through each section, trying to cover everything in half the time. That is, do not try to cram two 2-hour sessions into only two hours. Each section has already been compacted as much as possible; setting out to do one in less than the recommended time is probably going to mean that rather than understanding one section entirely, you don't understand two sections at all.

Extra Time. What do you do if you have extra time? Maybe you will find that you enjoy studying this material and would like to have more. Maybe you will find that you have unexpectedly obtained more time (a snowstorm closes your school for the day; a kind boss gives you some time off). You should take advantage of your extra time in one of the following ways.

1. *Memorize key concepts and have a friend quiz you on them.* If you have extra time, you may be able to memorize more math rules or more grammar concepts. Most persons who have only 10 hours to study have to be content with understanding all the rules and memorizing the most important ones; with extra time you can go back and memorize all of the rules.

2. *Retake the practice exams offered at the end of each section.* Answer *all* of the questions, not just the ones you missed the first time through. As you answer each question, ask yourself what concept it was testing, and what specific piece of information you needed to answer it. You may be pleasantly surprised later to find that questions on the actual SAT are very, very similar to questions found in these materials.

3. *Review outside materials.* Supplementary reading is to be done *only* if you have already completed all 10 hours of study. It is *supplementary*, meaning that it is in addition to your basic study plan. Do not spend time on supplementary materials in lieu of your regular study materials.

So far, so good. You have now set aside time for studying. You have some idea how to salvage the situation if you get behind in your studies, and how best to use any additional time you may have. You are ready for the last step in these introductory materials: the preview.

Exercise Two: Previewing

To preview material is to skim through it, finding salient points. Take a few minutes now to go back and read the Table of Contents. See what this book has to offer besides the five two-hour study sessions. Note the appendix. Now flip through the body of the book, seeing how it is set up. By doing so, you will be more comfortable with the material when you are actually ready to sit down and begin working on it. By the way, previewing is an excellent skill to develop and use on the actual SAT. More will be discussed on that point in the next section, which you are ready to turn to now.

(NOTE: You were allotted an hour for this Introduction. How are you doing for time? You probably took much less than an hour, in which case you may take a break, or go directly to the next hour's material.)

Hour Two: The SAT

Set Your Clock. *You should have finished the Introduction in one hour or less. You are allotted a full hour for studying this section.*

What You Will See

The SAT is a 6-section exam, with all questions in the multiple-choice format. You will not have to write an essay or give a timed writing sample. The sections are as follows:

Two Verbal Sections
Two Math Sections
One Grammar (Test of Standard Written English) Section
One Experimental Section

The Verbal Sections. You will have two verbal sections. One section will have 45 questions. There will be 15 antonyms, 10 sentence completions, 10 analogies, and 10 reading comprehension questions. The other verbal section will have 40 questions. There will be 10 antonyms, 5 sentence completions, 10 analogies, and 10 reading comprehension questions.

In both sections, these questions will be in no particular order. Generally, the section begins with antonyms; however, the remaining question types may be in any order, such as sentence completion–analogies–reading comprehension or analogies–reading comprehension–sentence completion. In tomorrow's lesson, you are given detailed information on question styles and instruction on how best to approach the questions.

The Math Sections. You will have two math sections. The first section will have 25 problem solving questions and no quantitative comparison questions. The other section will have 35 questions. There will be 20 quantitative comparison questions and 15 problem solving questions.

In the section with both quantitative comparison and problem solving questions, generally the order is seven problem solving questions, 20 quantitative comparison questions, eight problem solving questions.

In the lesson for Day Four, you are given detailed information on each question type along with suggestions on how to approach the questions.

The Grammar Section. The grammar section is known as the Test of Standard Written English (TSWE). "Standard written English" is the name given to a specific type of formal grammar used in writing as opposed to speaking. This section has 50 questions. Thirty-five of the questions are on usage; the remaining 15 questions are on sentence correction. The lessons on Day Five give detailed information on each question type along with suggestions on how to approach the questions.

The Experimental Section. The experimental section will be either verbal, mathematical, or TSWE. Therefore, if you have three verbal sections, for example, you know that one of them is experimental. However, you do *not* know which one of the three is experimental; therefore, you should do your best on all three. Do not try to outsmart the test makers and guess which section is experimental.

The experimental section does not count toward your score. In fact, your score report does not even give you information on how well or poorly you did in this section.

Timing

For every section, regardless of what subject matter it covers or how many questions it has, you are given 30 minutes. Since there are six sections, the total exam takes three hours.

Ordering of Sections

The sections may be given to you in any order. Within any test room, different students will be given different exam formats. That means that you may be working on a verbal section while the person next to you is working on a math section. Remember that you are only allowed to work on one section at a time; you may not finish early on a verbal section and go back to do some more work on a math section.

Determination of Your Score

You are penalized for random guessing on the SAT. You receive +1 point for every question you answer correctly, 0 points for every question you do not answer, and either −¼ or −⅓ point for every question you answer incorrectly. If the question has five possible answers, A-B-C-D-E, you lose ¼ point for a wrong answer. If the question has only four possible answers, A-B-C-D, you lose ⅓ point for a wrong answer. The only question style on the SAT with only four answer choices is quantitative comparisons. All other question styles have five possible answers.

Your SAT score will be reported on a range of 200–800. You get 200 points automatically; you cannot get a lower score. An 800 is the highest possible score. You will receive two 200–800 scores, one for the two verbal sections combined and one for the two math sections combined.

Within the verbal section, you will receive two subscores. These scores will be given for reading comprehension and vocabulary and are based on a 20–80 (rather than 200–800) range.

The TSWE is given a score based on 20–60+. This score is often considered separately by colleges and universities, and is not considered a part of the actual SAT. Frequently, schools use the TSWE score only to help place students in the proper level English classes. Occasionally, a "borderline" college applicant will be admitted or rejected on the basis of the TSWE score.

There is no passing or failing score on the SAT. There is also no "curve"; your performance is yours alone. How well or poorly other students did is not reflected in your numerical score. You are, however, compared to other students via a percentile rank. This rank tells you the percentage of students in a given group whose scores were below yours. For example, if your percentile rank is 91, then 91% of the people in the group had a lower score than you did.

NOTE: This discussion of scoring has been just a brief overview. If you want more information, there is an excellent discussion along with a sample copy of an actual score report in the book, *10 SATs*. The book was released by the College Entrance Examination Board and may be found in most bookstores.

The Score Report

Approximately six weeks after you have taken the exam, you will be sent a score report. This is a small piece of paper giving the scores discussed above. This score report will also be sent to the colleges and universities you specify; no report will be released without your written permission.

Using the Scores

Colleges and universities vary greatly in the use they make of your SAT scores. Some consider the SAT score almost exclusively in determining whether to admit you; some use it in conjunction with your grades; some consider it only if you are a "borderline" applicant. You definitely should call or write to your school before taking the SAT to find out how important your test score will be to your application. NOTE: Chances are that you will be applying to more than one school. Do not assume that all schools have the same policy, or that you will get into the school of your choice. Contact each school.

Scoring Cancellation and Errors

If you want to cancel your score, you may fill out a cancellation form before leaving the test room. If you want to cancel after the test, you must follow a detailed procedure outlined in the SAT *Student Bulletin* (discussed later). If you feel there has been a scoring error (highly unlikely since all exams are machine scored), you may request the SAT Score Verification Service. Contact

Educational Testing Service (ETS) for more information on this service (for which you are charged an additional fee).

Repeating the Exam

You may take the exam as often as you like. In fact, many teachers recommend that students take the test each time it is given from the time they are sophomores until they are seniors. Some schools look only at your highest score; some schools look to see whether you have improved or done worse; some schools average the scores. Contact each school directly to find out its policy.

For More Information

This introduction has only given general information most students need to know. If you are in a special situation (such as being a handicapped student) or want more detailed information on any topic, you may want to pick up the SAT *Student Bulletin*. This is a small booklet distributed free by the College Board and ETS. You may obtain a copy of the bulletin at most high schools or junior colleges. If you cannot find a copy, you may obtain one directly from the College Board by writing to

College Board ATP
CN 6200
Princeton, New Jersey
08541-6200

If you prefer to call, you may telephone one of the two following numbers.

Princeton, New Jersey: (609) 771-7600
     (8:30 A.M. to 9:30 P.M.)
Berkeley, California: (415) 849-0950
     (8:15 A.M. to 4:30 P.M.)

NOTE: The bulletin discussed above is also the Application Booklet; you may have already been given one by your guidance counselor. While the bulletin is valuable, there is a lot of information in it that you may not need (such as on how to register to take the exam if you are overseas); you may not have the time to go through it entirely.

2.

DAY TWO

Hour One: Antonyms and Analogies

Set Your Clock. *You will have a full hour to learn about the first two (out of four) question types found in the verbal ability section of the SAT. These questions are antonyms and analogies. The remaining two verbal question types, sentence completion and reading comprehension, will be covered in the second hour of today's lesson.*

What You Will See

The Verbal Ability section has 45 questions. Generally, fifteen of those are antonyms and ten are analogies.

Antonyms. Each antonym question consists of two parts: the word being tested and five answer choices. The word being tested will be printed all in capital letters; the answer choices will be in lower case letters.

EXAMPLE: LISTLESS: A. restless B. energetic C. creative
D. uneducated E. rude

Analogies. Each analogy question consists of two parts: the test pair of words and the five answer pairs. The test pair of words will be printed all in capital letters; the answer choices will be in lower case letters.

EXAMPLE: HAIRY:BALD:: A. tall:slender B. female:feminine
C. slovenly:messy D. ecstatic:miserable
E. successful:wealthy

Ordering the Questions

In the verbal section, generally the antonyms and analogies are not the first two question types. In fact, it is not uncommon to find the analogies at the very end of the section. Often the order of the questions is: antonyms, sentence completions, reading comprehension, and analogies. *Regardless of the order in which the question types are presented, do the antonyms first.* Answering an antonym question takes very little time. You only have to read a total of six words. In the time that it would take you to read one reading comprehension question, or one sentence completion question, you might read and answer all 15 antonyms. Therefore, by doing the antonyms first, you are making the wisest use of your time.

NOTE: Be very careful when you skip around within a section to keep track of your answers in the proper spaces on your answer grid. If you are doing analogies which are questions 36–45, be certain you are filling in answer ovals 36–45, not 16–25.

How to Do the Questions

Antonyms. With an antonym question, you should do the following:

1. *Read the question word.* This seems obvious and simple, but you must be careful of one thing: read the word that is actually printed, not the word you want to see. For example, you may see the word "designated" but accidentally read "designed." When you go to look for an antonym, you may become totally confused and frustrated because there is no word that means the opposite of "designed." Then, after becoming irritated and wasting precious time trying to force one of the answers to meet your needs, you have to go back and reread the word as it should have been read the first time. Take your time reading each question.

2. *Define the question word.* Before you look at the answer choices, ask yourself what the question word means. For example, if the word is "listless," you know that it means "lethargic, lacking energy, slow-moving." Don't worry about finding "precise" defini-

tions; the only one who knows what you are thinking is yourself. If the word is an adjective but you define it as a noun, that's fine, as long as you get the general meaning. If you can't think of an exact definition, but have a hazy idea of what the word means from having seen it used in some context, fine. How you define the word is up to you. Just do take the time to think about what the word means *before* going on to the next step.

3. *Predict the answer.* An antonym is a word meaning "opposite." When you are looking for an antonym, you are looking for a word that means the opposite of your question word. Since you have already defined listless to yourself, you can go ahead and predict a word that is the opposite. If you defined listless as "lacking energy," it is a simple step to predict that an opposite is "having energy," or "energetic." Again, don't worry about finding exactly the right word or exactly the right form; simply get a general idea of what a possible antonym would be.

4. *Look for the answer.* Now that you have predicted that the answer is "energetic," read the answer choices to determine whether that exact answer or one similar in meaning to it is given. If you note the example given earlier in this section, "energetic" is answer choice B. By defining the word and predicting its *opposite*, you have taken the quickest and most accurate route to obtaining an answer.

5. *Check your answer.* Most of the time, the word you predict as an antonym will in fact be given in the answer choices and will be the correct answer. The vast majority of the time you may feel confident that your prediction is correct; trust yourself. However, if you are uncertain of your definition, or you have a little extra time, you may want to read the other four answer choices to be absolutely certain that there is no other answer that is a little "more correct," one that seems to be a slightly better opposite. For example, if you were looking for the opposite of white, gray would be right, but black would be "more right." Generally, however, you do *not* want to spend a lot of time thinking about all of the answer choices. If you have predicted an answer that is given as an answer choice, you should go on to the next question.

What Do I Do When. . . ?

Suppose that you have followed all of the steps above very carefully. You took your time reading the word so that you didn't make a careless error. You defined the word, predicted its antonym, and looked at the answer key, only to find there is no answer there remotely resembling what you had hoped to find! Now what?

Now you do two things. First, *review your question.* Go back and reread the question word to make absolutely certain you read it correctly. Redefine it in your mind, to make certain that you used a good definition. Try to remember where, in what context, you have seen the word used. Predict an answer again. Check the answer choices again. *Be certain that you are matching the right answer choices to the right question word.* Occasionally, a student will read (for example) question 36 but look at the answer choices for question 37. Be very careful not to make such careless errors.

If you are positive you have made no "technical" errors, the next step is to use the answer choices. Read all five of the answer choices. If two or more words are synonyms (words that mean the same thing), both those words must be wrong. This is because two answers cannot be correct; therefore, neither one is correct. Using this tip will help you eliminate two out of the five answers.

Next, try to look at the prefixes of the words. Although you may be trapped on occasion by (for example) a word that begins with "mal" (meaning "bad") and a word that begins with "bene," (meaning "good") that are not antonyms, generally using prefixes will be helpful.

Analogies. With an analogy question you should do the following:

1. *Read the question words.* As with the antonyms, take the time to read the words that are actually printed. Do not subconsciously substitute words of your own.

2. *Find the relationship between the question words.* This step is the heart of the entire analogies process. An analogy is a comparison between two things, a likening of one thing to another. When you

see an analogy, ask yourself what the *relationship* is between the items. Is one a part of the other? Did one occur earlier in time than the other? Does one follow the other? If you properly define the relationship between the items, you will get the answer correct.

There are several basic relationships that are found on this exam. While these are by no means all of the relationships that may be tested, many questions use these.

PART–WHOLE

EXAMPLE: QUESTION:EXAM. A question is a part or portion of an exam.

EXAMPLE: STEM:FLOWER. A stem is a part of a flower.

COMPONENT–PRODUCT

EXAMPLE: BUTTER:CAKE. Butter is a component, an ingredient of a cake (the cake is the product).

EXAMPLE: CHIP:COMPUTER. A chip is a component of a computer (the computer is the product).

SYNONYMS

EXAMPLE: HAIRY:HIRSUTE. To be hairy or covered with hair is the same as to be hirsute.

EXAMPLE: ARROGANT:HAUGHTY. To be arrogant or conceited is the same as to be haughty.

ANTONYMS

EXAMPLE: LANGUID:FRENETIC. To be languid is to be listless, nonenergetic. To be frenetic is to be very energetic, active.

EXAMPLE: KNOTTY:SIMPLE. To be knotty is to be difficult and complex (such as a knotty problem).

CAUSE–EFFECT

EXAMPLE: OVEREAT:OBESITY. To overeat is to become obese (fat); overeating is the cause, obesity is the result or effect.

EXAMPLE: SABOTAGE:DISASTER. To sabotage something is to harm or hinder it, possibly leading to disaster. Sabotage is the cause; disaster is the effect.

CHARACTERISTIC

EXAMPLE: WATER:POTABLE. Water has the characteristic of being potable (drinkable).

EXAMPLE: CLICHÉ:HACKNEYED. A cliché, a statement or saying that has been overused, has the characteristic of being hackneyed, of being trite or lacking in originality and freshness.

PROGRESSION

EXAMPLE: JUNIOR:SENIOR. A junior who performs well in school progresses to becoming a senior.

EXAMPLE: BOY:MAN. A boy becomes a man.

3. *Choose the answer with the same relationship.* Once you have determined the relationship between the words in the question, look for a pair of words in the answers that has that same relationship. Note that the *meanings* of the words are irrelevant. If the question words are about baboons but have the relationship of cause-effect, it makes no difference that the answer words are about scientists. As long as the *relationship* is correct, your answer is correct.

What Do I Do When...?

If you have followed the above steps but cannot seem to find a correct answer, go back through the same steps again. Much, if not most, of the time, the problem lies in sheer carelessness. Did you read the question words incorrectly? Did you choose the wrong relationship? Did you look at the answers to the wrong question? Take the time to go back through the process one more time.

If you cannot find the relationship between the words in the question because you don't know what those words mean, guess at an answer if "the odds are with you" (remember that you lose ¼ point for every wrong answer; you probably should not guess unless you can eliminate at least one and preferably two answer choices) and go on. Don't waste your time trying to analyze an answer. For example, suppose the question words are IRASCI-BLE:CHOLERIC. If you don't know what even one of the words (let alone both!) means, there is no way you can find an answer. As far as you know they could be synonyms (true: each means grouchy, irritable), antonyms, or virtually anything else.

Traps to Avoid

With antonyms, there are three basic traps to avoid:

1. *Do not misread the word.* As discussed earlier, it is very, very easy to transpose a few letters and (for example) make "angle" out of "angel." Take the time to read the question word carefully.

2. *Remember to choose an antonym.* Many persons who make mistakes in this section do so because they define the word, then look for that definition among the answer choices. You want an *opposite*, not a synonym. Often you will find that synonyms *are* given as answer choices; don't let them trap you.

3. *Keep track of your numbering.* With these short questions, it is easy to make numerical mistakes twice, once on the questions (where you read question 36 but the answers for question 37) and once on the answer grid (where you fill in ovals 1–10, rather than 36–45).

With analogy questions, there are three basic traps to avoid:

1. *Do not misread the words.* Unfortunately, people tend to read the first word, then predict the second word. For example, if the

first word is "man," many people think that the second word must be "woman." They play "word association" games, rather than reading what the question has. Take the time to do a careful reading.

2. *Do not choose an answer with a reversed relationship.* This is perhaps the most common error in this section. If the question is BOY:MAN, the answer *cannot* be WOMAN:GIRL. The relationship would be one of progression; a boy grows into a man. A woman does not grow into a girl; the relationship there is backwards.

3. *Do not choose answers based on the meanings of the words.* If the questions are about computers, the answer may very easily be about chocolate cake. The meanings themselves are irrelevant; you are only concerned with the relationships between the pairs of words.

Time-saving Suggestions

Antonyms

1. *Do the antonyms first.* Each antonym only requires a few seconds to read and answer.

2. *Predict and look for an answer.* You save much time if you already have an idea of what you are looking for, rather than just moseying through the answer choices. Once you find the answer you have predicted, you may go on to the next question. You really don't have to look through the rest of the answers unless you were somewhat insecure about your definition, or you have extra time.

3. *Guess wisely.* If you have absolutely no idea what a word means, don't worry and fret over it, trying to analyze it. Unless you know that the meaning is on the tip of your tongue, so to speak, don't think about it. With many antonyms, either you know them immediately, or you don't. If you are going to guess (always keeping in mind the penalty for a wrong answer), do so quickly; otherwise go on to the next question.

Analogies

1. *Do the analogies second.* Each analogy should only take you a few seconds to read and answer.

2. *Define the relationship as quickly as possible.* If you have memorized the relationships given above, you will find that many questions will demonstrate one of them. If the question words do not fit neatly into a specific relationship, create your own with a sentence, such as ESKIMO:SUNBURN. "An Eskimo is *unlikely* to get sunburn."

3. *Guess wisely.* As always, if you have no idea what one or both of the words mean, go on to the next question. Do not waste your time trying to analyze it, or staring at it as if the meaning of a word you have never seen before will suddenly pop into your mind. If the word is familiar (you have seen it before but can't quite remember what it means), then it might be worth a moment of thought. However, if you didn't even know that such a word existed ("multifariousness?!"), go on to the next question.

Practice Exam: Antonyms and Analogies

Please take the following practice exam on antonyms and analogies. The verbal ability section of the actual exam has 45 questions; these 15 antonyms and 10 analogies are representative of a portion of that section. An answer key and explanatory answers follow. Score yourself and remember: Incorrect answers cost you ¼ point each!

Antonyms

DIRECTIONS: Each question consists of a word printed in capital letters and five words printed in lower case letters. Choose the word or group of words that is most nearly *opposite* in meaning to the word printed in capital letters. Circle the letter that appears before your choice.

1. AUSTERE: A. somber B. gaudy C. quiet D. insignificant
   E. haughty

2. INCENSED: A. pleased B. overpriced C. obedient D. typical
   E. anonymous

3. ORTHODOX: A. miniature B. self-sufficient C. synonymous
   D. unusual E. understated

4. THWART: A. combine B. dissemble C. aid D. panic E. split

5. ACCOST: A. replace B. avoid C. trust D. price E. renew

6. CAPITULATE: A. resist B. surrender C. whisper D. object
   E. dishearten

7. DISREPUTE: A. munificence B. respect C. ignorance
   D. animation E. luck

8. EFFRONTERY: A. shyness B. criticism C. aptitude D. fervor
   E. originality

9. INFAMY: A. pessimism B. jeopardy C. disgrace D. glory
   E. drunkenness

10. SOLICIT: A. twitch B. rant C. carp D. tense E. donate

11. PROVINCIAL: A. sophisticated B. tranquil C. evasive
    D. flagrant E. ridiculous

12. GULLIBLE: A. honorable B. inopportune C. voluminous
    D. credulous E. disbelieving

13. METICULOUS: A. haphazard B. reverent C. conceited
    D. adroit E. feminine

14. PRECOCIOUS: A. slow to mature B. easy to command
    C. unable to be understood D. difficult to explain E. hard to
    do

15. RESPLENDENT: A. inanimate B. emotional C. somber
    D. secretive E. masculine

Analogies

DIRECTIONS: Each question consists of a pair of words printed in
capital letters and five pairs of words printed in lower case letters.
Find the relationship between the words printed in capital letters.
Then choose from among the words printed in lower case letters
that pair which most nearly has the same relationship. Circle the
letter that appears before your choice.

1. RAZOR : BARBER ::
   A. knife : butcher   D. chalk : singer
   B. brush : sculptor   E. wrench : carpenter
   C. logger : saw

2. BEVY : QUAILS ::
   A. choir : conductors   D. cattle : herd
   B. pride : lions   E. garden : trees
   C. covey : bees

3. SCRUTINIZE : IGNORE ::
   A. attempt : try   D. visualize : see
   B. succeed : success   E. laud : denigrate
   C. aid : abet

4. ALWAYS : FREQUENTLY ::
   A. sometimes : never   D. customary : usual
   B. unique : unusual   E. early : late
   C. wonderful : perfect

5. TEXTURE : TOUCH ::
   A. sound : ear   D. scent : odor
   B. color : see   E. smooth : rough
   C. tongue : flavor

6. POET : WRITER ::
   A. principal : teacher
   B. athlete : coach
   C. scientist : engineer
   D. neurologist : doctor
   E. artist : painter

7. ANTENNA : TELEVISION ::
   A. nostril : nose
   B. envelope : letter
   C. keyboard : computer
   D. tablecloth : table
   E. couch : dust

8. GROUSE : COMPLAIN ::
   A. relax : work
   B. smile : laugh
   C. laud : praise
   D. sleep : snore
   E. ignore : attend

9. ICEBOX : REFRIGERATOR ::
   A. velocipede : bicycle
   B. dictionary : encyclopedia
   C. cold : cool
   D. stereo : record player
   E. bed : crib

10. BUTTONS : SHIRT ::
    A. zipper : snaps
    B. clasp : necklace
    C. door : knob
    D. shoes : laces
    E. glasses : face

ANTONYMS ANSWER KEY

1. B	5. B	9. D	13. A
2. A	6. A	10. E	14. A
3. D	7. B	11. A	15. C
4. C	8. A	12. E	

Explanations

1. **(B)** *Austere* means unadorned, somber. "The interrogation room had an *austere* appearance, containing only one chair,

one overhead light, and dark grey walls." The opposite is decorated, bright, gaudy.

2. **(A)** *Incensed* means aroused, angered. "Donald was *incensed* when he found that he would have to share billing with his rival, Daffy Duck." The opposite is pleased, happy.

3. **(D)** *Orthodox* means conforming to established doctrine and practice, conventional. "The conservative teacher used only *orthodox* teaching methods, which made him much less interesting than other teachers who often tried something new." The opposite is not conventional, unusual.

4. **(C)** *Thwart* means to oppose successfully, to frustrate. "Robin Hood was able to *thwart* all of the sheriff's attempts to capture and imprison him." The opposite is to help, to aid.

5. **(B)** *Accost* means to approach in an aggressive way, to solicit. "Pete the Panhandler *accosted* only well-dressed people, asking them for spare change." The opposite is to avoid, to ignore.

6. **(A)** *Capitulate* means to stop resisting, to surrender. "After weeks of negotiation, the rebels decided to *capitulate*, but only because their food supplies were severely diminished." The opposite is to resist, to fight against.

7. **(B)** *Disrepute* means a state of being held in low esteem, a state of disgrace. "The teacher was held in *disrepute* by his peers because he refused to go on strike with them." The opposite is respect, admiration.

8. **(A)** *Effrontery* means shameless boldness, insolence. "Believe it or not, Snow White had the *effrontery* to ask for her money back, saying the apple tasted funny!" The opposite is shyness, a lack of aggressiveness.

9. **(D)** *Infamy* means disgrace, dishonor, a very bad reputation. "The *infamy* of the outlaw had preceded her, causing the townsfolk to run and hide when they saw Black Bertha coming." The opposite is glory, a good reputation.

10. **(E)** *Solicit* means to entreat, to beg, to approach with a request or plea. "Each year policewoman Sandi would *solicit* people

on her beat, asking them to buy tickets to the Police Officers Ball." The opposite is to donate, to give.

11. **(A)** *Provincial* means limited in outlook, unsophisticated. "At its weekly meeting, the City Snobs club decided not to admit Mr. Bucolic, claiming that he was too *provincial* to become a member of the club." The opposite is sophisticated, worldly.

12. **(E)** *Gullible* means easily deceived or duped, naive. "Famous circus owner P. T. Barnum believed that there were *gullible* people everywhere." The opposite is disbelieving, not easily deceived.

13. **(A)** *Meticulous* means careful, attentive to even the smallest detail. "Because Stefan was a *meticulous* person naturally, the Secret Service asked him to be a code breaker in World War II." The opposite is careless, haphazard.

14. **(A)** *Precocious* means exhibiting adult qualities at an early age. "The casting director thought the part was difficult and was looking for an especially *precocious* child to play the lead." The opposite is immature, not as sophisticated as others of that age group.

15. **(C)** *Resplendent* means illustrious, bright. "Miss Dietrich was *resplendent* in her shimmering sequined gown under the lights." The opposite is somber, dark, dull.

ANALOGIES ANSWER KEY

1. A	4. B	7. D	9. A
2. B	5. B	8. C	10. B
3. E	6. D		

Explanations

1. **(A)** A *razor* is a tool customarily used by a *barber* in the pursuit of his trade (he uses a razor to shave customers). A knife is customarily used by a butcher in the pursuit of his trade (he uses the knife to cut meat). Note that answer C might be correct but is backwards. Answers B, D, and E all have "tools" that are not customarily used by the persons involved (e.g., a

sculptor would use a chisel, not a brush; a painter would use a brush).

2. **(B)** A group of *quails* is called a *bevy;* a group of lions is called a pride. Note that answer D might be correct but is backwards. Answers A, C, and E are not logical. A group of singers, not conductors, is a choir. A covey is a flock or brood of birds, not bees. A garden is not a group of trees; a "forest" might be the correct term for such a group.

3. **(E)** To *scrutinize* is to look at or examine very carefully. It is the opposite of to *ignore.* Answer E has the same relationship of opposites; to laud is to praise, while to denigrate is to criticize, to belittle.

4. **(B)** The relationship is one of intensity or strength; *always* is a so-called *perfect* word, meaning that it is without exception. "Frequently" is a less strong version. Something that is done frequently has an exception. In answer B, "unique" is a "perfect" word; if something is unique, it is the only one. Something that is unusual is not the only one, it is simply one of a few. Note that the relationship is one of stronger to weaker, so that answers A and C are backwards. Answer D has synonyms; answer E has antonyms. Do not confuse relationships of degree (that is, words which are greater/lesser or stronger/weaker) with antonyms or synonyms.

5. **(B)** This was a difficult question to put into a specific category; you should have used the words in a sentence. You find the *texture* of something by *touch*ing it; you find the color of something by seeing it. Note that answer A would be correct if it read "sound:hear" rather than "sound:ear."

6. **(D)** A *poet* is a type of *writer,* a specific category of writer. A neurologist is a type or specific category of doctor. Answers C and E might be correct, but are backwards.

7. **(D)** This is a position relationship; an *antenna* goes on top of a *television.* A tablecloth goes on top of a table. Note that answer E is more logical if considered "backward"; dust probably would be below or beneath a couch, not on top of it.

8. **(C)** To *grouse* is to *complain;* the words are synonyms. Answer C has synonyms as well; to laud is to praise. Note that answers A and E have antonyms (opposites), not synonyms.

9. **(A)** This is a "time" relationship. The early *refrigerators* were called *iceboxes;* early bicycles or tricycles were called velocipedes. Answer E might be considered correct, but is backwards ("stereo" is a more modern term than "record player"). Answer C is trying to trap you with the substantive meaning of the words, making you think that temperature has something to do with the answers. Remember to choose answers based on relationships, not on meanings.

10. **(B)** *Buttons* are a part of a shirt with the specific function of opening and closing the *shirt.* A clasp is a part of a necklace with the specific function of opening and closing the necklace. Note that answers C and D might be correct, but are backwards.

NUMBER RIGHT:＿＿(Give yourself one point for each.)

NUMBER WRONG:＿＿(Multiply by ¼ point each.)

FINAL SCORE:＿＿(Subtract the second number from the first; you may have an answer with a fraction, such as 18¾.)

Hour Two: Sentence Completion and Reading Comprehension

Set Your Clock. You should have finished the first half of this day's work (the section on "Antonyms and Analogies") in one hour. If you finished early, you may take a break before beginning this section or you may begin immediately. You are allotted a full hour for studying this section.

What You Will See

The verbal ability section has 45 questions. Generally, ten of those are sentence completion and ten are reading comprehension. NOTE: One of the verbal sections has only 40, not 45, questions. The 40-question section will have five sentence completion and 10 reading comprehension questions.

Sentence Completion. Each sentence completion question consists of a full sentence with one or two blanks. Following the sentence are five answer choices containing a word or words to fit in the blank or blanks.

EXAMPLE: Although her doctor recommended that she _____ from talking so much, Frances was unable to _____ calling her best friend to tell her all the details of her date.

A. abstain . . . resist

B. stop . . . eschew

C. desist . . . stop

D. refrain . . . halt

E. keep . . . be

Reading Comprehension. Each reading comprehension "question" consists of two parts: the reading comprehension passage and a specific question based on information given or implied in that particular passage. Below an example is given of such a question; examples of the reading passages will be given in the practice exam later in these materials.

EXAMPLE: According to the passage, which of the following is true of Mount Klyuchevskaya?

A. It is in the capital city of Siberia.
B. It is in the central Siberian highlands.
C. It has the highest elevation of any place in Siberia.
D. It is the highest mountain in Russia.
E. All of the above.

Ordering the Questions. You learned in the first hour of this lesson that you should do the antonyms first, then the analogies. After you have done those two question types, you should do the sentence completion and reading comprehension questions. Therefore, regardless of the order the questions are given in the section, you should answer them in the following order:

• Antonyms
• Analogies
• Sentence Completion
• Reading Comprehension

You should do the sentence completion questions third because they require some time to read and think about. You have to read a complete sentence (as opposed to just a word or two words in the antonym and analogy questions) and think about it as an entity, try to make sense of it. Then you have to read the answer choices, and consider how well or poorly they would fit into the sentence. This often means that you end up reading the sentence several times, once with each answer choice inserted. Since this is relatively time consuming, save it for near the end.

NOTE: Because the sentence completion questions are familiar and comfortable (these are the type of "fill in the blank" questions you have probably seen throughout your school years), you may be tempted to do them first. You may even feel that since you can get most of these right, and may not do nearly so well on the antonyms, these are your first priority. You may be correct that in terms of *percentages* you do the best on these. However, in the time it takes you to do one or two sentence correction questions, you could have done *all* of the antonyms and some of the analogies. Even if you miss several of those questions, your overall score may be better than it would be with just the sentence completion questions. Therefore, force yourself to do the sentence completion questions *after* the antonyms and analogies.

The reading comprehension questions definitely should be done last. Each question generally takes significantly longer to do than does any question of any other type. You have to read the entire passage, then read the question, then *read all the answer choices* (because often reading comprehension questions have answers such as "all of the above" or "none of the above"). Doing all of this takes quite a while. If you begin with the reading comprehension questions, you may never get to some of the other questions. If you begin with the other questions, you may not be able to finish one or two reading comprehension questions, as opposed to all 15 of the antonyms or all 10 of the analogies.

NOTE: Be *very* careful when you skip around within a section to keep track of your answers in the proper spaces on your answer grid. If you are doing sentence completion questions which are (for example) questions 16–25, be certain that you are filling in answer ovals 16–25, not 26–35.

How to Do the Questions

Sentence Completions. With a sentence completion question, you should do the following:

1. *Read the entire sentence through before looking at the answers.* Read the sentence to yourself, saying "blank" where the space is. In other words, you would say, "Although her doctor recommended that she *blank* from talking so much, Frances was unable to *blank* calling her best friend to tell her all the details of her date." If you read the answer words before you read the sentence or try to read them in conjunction with your first reading of the sentence, you will confuse yourself. Try to get the sense of the sentence first.

2. *Predict what words will fill in the blanks.* If you have read the sentence through and understood the gist of it, you should be able to predict what word or words will fit it. Don't spend a great deal of time trying to predict an exact word; just get the general idea, the connotation, of what is needed.

3. *Look for your prediction.* Very, very often you will find that the words you predicted are in the answer choices. Much of the time your predictions will be exactly correct. If the words you predicted are not given, look for their synonyms.

4. *Check your answer.* You must go back and reread the entire sentence with your choice inserted. This step *cannot* be eliminated. If you reread the entire sentence, you will catch any errors or traps given. If you do not, you may later find that the first blank was correctly filled but that the second one confused the sentence entirely.

Reading Comprehension. With a reading comprehension question, you should do the following:

1. *Preview the passage.* Take just a few seconds to skim through the first and last paragraphs of *all* the passages. This brief reading will allow you to determine the passage type to which each belongs. You will probably encounter at least one example of each of the three basic types of reading passages: detail or factual (in which many specific facts or statistics are given), chronological (in which a progression of events is discussed), and theoretical (in which a theory is advanced or a hypothesis discussed).

2. *Order your passages.* You may find that you are better at reading, understanding, and answering questions on one type of passage than on another. For example, you may find that you are very good at "reading between the lines" and understanding theories, but that you cannot stand to read a dry passage filled with dates and numbers. In such a case, you would read and answer questions on a theoretical passage first, and save a detailed or factual passage for the end. By ordering the passage types you help yourself to do first those you are best at. Thus, if you run out of time, you have left only those questions which you least enjoy and probably would have done the worst on anyway.

3. *Read and notate the passages.* You do not want to do a great deal of underlining and circling; you are not going to have to come back and take a semester final on this material someday! You will have the material right in front of you to refer to as you go through the questions. However, if, as you read through a pas-

sage, you want to circle a particular definition which you think may be asked about, or you want to number the steps in a progression, doing so will take but a few seconds. Remember that once you begin underlining, you may find that *everything* looks important, so that you are basically underlining almost the whole passage. If you are generally the underlining type, you may try to satisfy your urges by instead simply making short notes in the margin on the important point of each paragraph.

4. *Read each question and all of the answer choices.* Do not be tricked into choosing the first answer that seems right. Take the time to read all the answer choices because the question might have a later answer that says, "all of the above," or "answers A, C, and D," or something of that sort.

5. *Answer the question based on the preceding passage only.* Do not use information given in one passage to answer questions following a second passage; you may only use information from the passage directly before the questions. Do not use outside information, knowledge that you have yourself. If you do not remember the answer to the question, go back to the passage and look for it. If the question calls for you to make an inference (such as asking you what the tone of the author is), don't waste time going back to the passage (the answer won't be there). Instead, think about your answer for a moment, and choose the most likely choice given. Don't agonize too much over your choice on any given problem; go on to the next question.

Traps to Avoid

With the sentence completion questions, there are three basic traps to avoid.

1. *Don't read the answers before reading the sentence;* doing so will confuse you and prejudice your choice. Take the time to read the sentence through carefully and predict the answer.

2. *Don't stop after reading just one blank.* In other words, if there are two blanks to be filled, and the first word in the answer correctly fills the first one, don't automatically assume that that answer is correct. Frequently, answer choices do fill one blank correctly but

fill in the second blank incorrectly. Read and think about *both* words.

3.   *Don't go on to the next question immediately after choosing your answer.* You must take the time to reread the entire sentence with your answer choice words filled in. This last step is one that persons tend to skip "in the interest of time," only to find out later that they made ridiculous and careless errors that could have been easily prevented.

With the reading comprehension questions, there are three basic traps to avoid.

1.   *Use only information given in the immediately preceding passage.* Assume that whatever the passage states is correct (even if you know or believe the information to be incorrect or outdated) and answer your questions based on it. Do not read more into the passage than is printed there.

2.   *Be certain you answer exactly what the question is calling for.* If the question asks you who was the first person to explore Australia, do not tell who was the first person to explore Austria. It is often easy to misread the question and give a "correct" answer to an "incorrect" question.

3.   *Give the best answer.* Occasionally (especially on questions that call for deductions), you will find more than one "correct" answer. Choose the one that is "most correct." This means that you *must read all the answer choices* even if you think the first one you read could be correct.

Time-saving Suggestions

Sentence Completions

1.   *Do the sentence completion questions third.* These questions take much longer than the antonyms and analogies, but not as long as the reading comprehension questions.

2.   *Predict and look for an answer.* You save much time if you already have an idea of what you are looking for. Once you find the

answer you have predicted, quickly insert it into the sentence to double check it. You will be pleasantly surprised to find out how often you have predicted *exactly* the right answer.

3. *Guess wisely.* If you have no idea what the question means (some questions can be written in a very roundabout manner, making them hard to understand) let alone what the answer is, go on to the next question. Do not waste much time trying to analyze the question or staring at it as if the answer will appear due to your sheer willpower! If you think you can answer the question, spend a little time on it. However, if you are confused or lost, go on to the next question. Remember that random guessing can hurt you on this exam; you lose ¼ point for every wrong answer.

Reading Comprehension

1. *Preview all the passages first.* Doing so will allow you to know which passage to read first and which to save until the end.

2. *Do not do much underlining or circling.* If you want to make a special note, write a brief comment in the margin so that you can find a particular definition or point later if you are asked about it.

3. *Guess wisely.* If you can narrow the answers down to four or fewer, you may want to guess. However, remember that random guessing may cost you, because every incorrect answer causes ¼ point to be subtracted from your score.

Practice Exam: Sentence Completion and Reading Comprehension

Please take the following practice exam on sentence completion and reading comprehension. The verbal ability section of the actual exam has 45 questions; these 10 sentence completion and 10 reading comprehension questions are representative of a portion of that section. An answer key and explanatory answers follow. Score yourself and remember: Incorrect answers cost you ¼ point each!

Sentence Completion

DIRECTIONS: Each sentence below has one or two blanks indicating omissions of words or phrases. Choose the word or group of words from the five answer choices that best fits the meaning of the sentence. Circle the letter that appears before your choice.

1. When the young man saw the _____ woman across the room, he ran over to be the first to ask her to dance.

   A. alluring
   B. childish
   C. puerile
   D. jejune
   E. unsophisticated

2. The arrogance of the actor was wholly _____ as he was just a _____ and had not yet earned the right to be conceited.

   A. expected . . . tyro
   B. unwarranted . . . beginner
   C. ridiculous . . . veteran
   D. futile . . . fool
   E. ludicrous . . . thespian

3. Although she admitted to having made a(n) _____ on the playing field, Gabriella still _____ that she had almost single-handedly won the game for her team.

   A. goal . . . said
   B. mistake . . . denied
   C. blunder . . . maintained
   D. shot . . . asserted
   E. error . . . refused

4. The _____ remarks of the seemingly mature young man _____ his appearance and assured us that he was a callow youth after all.

   A. sophisticated . . . supported
   B. foolish . . . reinforced
   C. intelligent . . . mitigated
   D. inane . . . belied
   E. charming . . . denied

5. Because Alan had spoken so _____ of his ex-wife, we were all surprised to meet such a(n)_____ young lady.

   A. disparagingly . . . charming
   B. glowingly . . . adorable
   C. rudely . . . boorish
   D. scathingly . . . contemptible
   E. little . . . tall

6. No one can succeed merely by _____ those who are already successful; one must have some virtues of one's own.

   A. reading about   D. watching
   B. emulating   E. hearing about
   C. denying

7. The convicts decided to _____ their escape plans when they agreed that the route through the desert was not _____.

   A. implement . . . easy   D. publicize . . . possible
   B. drop . . . hard   E. eschew . . . impossible
   C. postpone . . . feasible

8. Despite Horace's _____, we decided that he was not capable of watching our children alone; therefore, we hired an additional _____.

   A. protests . . . person   D. entreaties . . . woman
   B. assurances . . . baby-sitter   E. past . . . one
   C. skills . . . child

9. A(n) _____ speaker, Chun Lee was often hired to _____ conventions.

   A. excellent . . . talk   D. poor . . . skip
   B. good . . . give   E. vehement . . . speak
   C. skilled . . . address

10. Dimitri _____ of his ability to get a date at the last minute; imagine his _____ when he had to go to the game alone!

   A. jeered . . . humiliation   D. boasted . . . embarrassment
   B. spoke . . . delight   E. bragged . . . success
   C. talked . . . enjoyment

Reading Comprehension

DIRECTIONS: Each passage is followed by questions pertaining to that passage. Read the passages and answer the questions based on information stated or implied in that passage.

Siberia (called Sibir in Russian) lies in Northern Asia. It is roughly divided into three areas: the central

Siberian uplands (with high plateaus that extend from the Lena to the Yenisey rivers), the west Siberian lowlands (with both forests and grasslands that stretch from the Yenisey River to the Ural Mountains), and the east Siberian highlands (containing Mount Klyuchevskaya, Siberia's highest point).

While most Siberians now are white Russians, some descendants of the original Mongolian settlers remain in the area. The Mongolians have long been noted for their raising of livestock, including goats and reindeer.

1. The best title for this passage may be

   A. The People of Siberia
   B. Siberian Agriculture
   C. Russians in Siberia
   D. An Introduction to Siberia
   E. The Criminals of Russia

2. This passage would most likely be found in which of the following?

   A. A Russian history book
   B. An encyclopedia
   C. A political treatise
   D. A travel brochure
   E. A sociology textbook

3. According to the passage, which of the following is true of Mount Klyuchevskaya?

   A. It is in the capital city of Russia.
   B. It is in the central Siberian highlands.
   C. It has the highest elevation of any place in Russia.
   D. It is the highest mountain in Russia.
   E. All of the above

4. Which of the following is a mountain range that may be found in Siberia?

   A. Klyuchevskaya   D. Ural
   B. Lena   E. None of the above
   C. Yenisey

The image that many persons have of a scientist is of a gray-haired old man with a bushy white mustache bending over test tubes, or of a young, balding man with thick spectacles, peering through a microscope. Few people think of women scientists, yet some of the most important persons in science have been female.

Dr. Florence Rena Sabin was elected to life membership in the New York Academy of Sciences, was a member of the Rockefeller Institute, and served as the president of the American Association of Anatomists. Dr. Sabin won recognition for her research work on tuberculosis, blood, and bone marrow, and was one of the first scientists to change the thrust of medicine from the cure of disease to the prevention of disease.

Dr. Gladys Anderson Emerson was the first scientist to isolate Vitamin E from wheat germ oil and study its functions. With a Ph.D. in nutrition and biochemistry from the University of California at Berkeley (awarded in 1932), Dr. Emerson became a major contributor to information about the effect and uses of vitamins within the human body. Particularly interested in the relationship between diet and cancer, Dr. Emerson was appointed a research associate at the Sloan-Kettering Institute for Cancer Research in New York City.

A Nobel Prize was awarded in 1964 to Dr. Dorothy Crowfoot Hodgkin, Chancellor of Bristol University in England. Dr. Hodgkin was a crystallographer who was given the prize in recognition of her skill in using X-ray techniques to determine the structure of chemical compounds, particularly penicillin. Dr. Hodgkin's Nobel Prize for Chemistry was the third one given to a woman. Previous recipients were Marie Curie in 1911 and Irene Joliot-Curie (the daughter of Marie Curie) in 1935. Both previous recipients had shared the prize with their husbands; Dr. Hodgkin was the first woman to be recognized without the help of her spouse.

Dr. Lise Meitner, a nuclear physicist born in 1878, was responsible for the introduction of the term "nuclear fission." Dr. Meitner studied under Dr. Max

Planck, originator of the quantum theory and winner of the Nobel Prize, and became his assistant at the University of Berlin. She was also a friend of Neils Bohr, another Nobel Prize winner. It was to Neils Bohr that Dr. Meitner relayed her theories that the atom could be split to give off immense amounts of energy. Bohr took the news to America and helped begin the experiments that were eventually to lead to the development of the atomic bomb.

5. According to the passage, the first female recipient of the Nobel Prize for Chemistry was

   A. Dr. Gladys Anderson Emerson
   B. Dr. Lise Meitner
   C. Marie Curie
   D. Dr. Dorothy Crowfoot Hodgkin
   E. Irene Joliot-Curie

6. Dr. Florence Rena Sabin is primarily remembered for her work with

   A. the prevention of disease
   B. Vitamin E and wheat germ oil
   C. atomic energy
   D. Niels Bohr
   E. cancer

7. The tone of this passage may best be described as

   A. sarcastic   D. whimsical
   B. incredulous   E. critical
   C. narrative

8. According to the passage, a crystallographer is

   A. one who grows crystals in a laboratory
   B. one who uses crystals in light and space experiments
   C. one who splits crystals into their smallest possible components
   D. one who charts the existence and frequency of crystals in nature
   E. the passage did not give a definition

Corporal punishment is a very emotional topic. Many persons firmly believe in the Biblical injunction "spare the rod and spoil the child," while others believe that those who are struck as children will grow up believing that violence is necessary to solve problems.

Only 50 years ago, children were regularly spanked in public schools and few persons protested. Now, if a child is spanked even for the most egregious violations, there may be lawsuits and criminal sanctions. Teachers and administrators must be very careful at all times to treat their charges with the same respect that they would show to adults. Striking a child even a mild blow in exasperation is forbidden by law in many cities and counties.

Teachers have difficulties at the other end of the spectrum as well. An instructor who hugs or strokes a child may be open to a charge of child abuse or sexual molestation. It is getting so bad that soon a teacher will not be able to touch or even talk to a child at all. Perhaps the time is right to introduce robots into the classroom.

9. The writer gives as an example of when a child might be struck as which of the following?

   A. when the child has not done his or her homework
   B. when the child has struck another child
   C. when the teacher is exasperated with the child
   D. when the teacher has been struck first by the child
   E. when the teacher has given several warnings to the child, all of which have been ignored

10. The writer mentions robots to make the point that
   A. soon teachers will be forced to function as unfeeling, uncaring robots
   B. soon students will be acting like robots
   C. robots are less likely to cause legal problems between teachers and parents
   D. robots are better teachers as they are less emotionally involved

E. robots are more easily trained to instruct without digression

SENTENCE COMPLETION ANSWER KEY

1. A	4. D	7. C	9. C
2. B	5. A	8. B	10. D
3. C	6. B		

Explanations

1. **(A)** If a young man *runs* all the way across a room to be the first to ask a woman to dance, that woman must be very attractive. "Alluring" means charming, enticing, attractive. The other answers are all somewhat similar in meaning to one another. Puerile and jejune mean unsophisticated, immature, childish. No one would run across a room to ask such a woman to dance.

2. **(B)** The second part of the sentence tells you that the actor had *not* yet earned the right to be conceited. Since arrogant means conceited, you know that he had not yet earned the right to be arrogant either, such that his arrogance was unwarranted, improper, undeserved. Since he had not *yet* earned the right to be conceited, he must be somewhat of a beginner, new to the business. Note that in answer A the second word, "tyro," which means a beginner or a novice, would be correct, but the first word is wrong.

3. **(C)** One admits to something poorly done, such as admitting to a blunder. A blunder is a mistake, an error. The word "although" tells you that regardless of that error, Gabriella still thinks she has done well. To *maintain* is to state definitely, to reiterate. Note that while answers B and E have words that make sense in the first blank, the words for the second blank would be illogical when put into the sentence. If you chose either of those answers, you were tricked. Don't forget to read *both* words in the answer and insert them into the sentence.

4. **(D)** The words "after all" at the end of the sentence tell you that while the man *looks* mature, he is immature or callow. Therefore, his remarks must have belied, or shown to be un-

ture, his seeming maturity. Remarks that show one to be immature must be ridiculous, foolish, or inane. Note that while answer B has a first word that could be correct, the second word is wrong.

5. **(A)** The key to this sentence is the word "surprised." You can deduce that the way Alan spoke of his ex-wife is the opposite of what she appeared to be to the speaker of the sentence. Therefore, the two blanks must have words that are somewhat opposite. Either he spoke well of her and she was unattractive, or he spoke ill of her and she was attractive. To speak disparagingly of someone is to speak ill of her, to criticize or belittle her. Note that answers B, C, and D are incorrect because they all have answers that follow logically from one another. For example, if one speaks glowingly of a woman, the listeners are not surprised to find that the woman is adorable. Answer E is somewhat humorous, but does not logically complete the sentence.

6. **(B)** The second half of the sentence says that one must have some virtues of one's own, meaning that one cannot simply copy the virtues of another. To emulate is to copy, to try to follow and be similar to.

7. **(C)** The key words are "route through the desert." You may infer that traveling through a desert is not the best way to go, so that a plan for doing so would not be practicable or feasible. Since such a route would not be feasible, the convicts would *postpone* their escape plans. Note that while the second word for answer A would be correct, the first word is wrong. To *implement* is to put in effect, to do.

8. **(B)** The key to this question is the second blank. Since the speaker does not think Horace is capable of watching children alone, there must be someone else hired. A person who watches children is a baby-sitter. Note that answers C and E both indicate that the speaker would be hiring a child to watch the children—not a logical situation. Answer D says "another" woman; it is safe to assume that Horace is a man's name. Answer A does not make as much sense in the first blank as does answer B.

9. **(C)** The second blank is the key to this question. Since Chun Lee is some sort of speaker, the second blank probably deals with speaking to or addressing a convention. Note that answers A and E both have grammatical problems: one talks or speaks *to* a convention. Without the word "to," the sentence is incorrect. Answer B does not make sense considering the word "speaker"; a good speaker does not give conventions, he speaks at them. Answer D is illogical; no one is hired to skip a convention.

10. **(D)** The end of the sentence says that Dimitri had to go to the game alone; probably he was not happy at having to do so. Therefore, you should predict that the second blank has a "negative" word, such as "humiliation" or "embarrassment." Answer A makes no sense; one does not "jeer of his ability."

READING COMPREHENSION ANSWER KEY

1. D	4. D	7. C	9. C
2. B	5. C	8. E	10. A
3. C	6. A		

Explanations

1. **(D)** The best title is one that summarizes the contents of the passage, but is neither too broad nor too specific. It gives a general idea of what the passage is going to contain, what concepts are going to be discussed. Answers A, B, and C, while discussed in the passage, are too specific to be a best title. Each is just one of several concepts covered. Answer E is not discussed at all.

2. **(B)** This passage gives a very brief overview of several factors about Siberia (such as its geography, people, and livestock). Such a brief summary would be found in an encyclopedia, where one goes to get an overall idea of a subject without going into a great many details. While history (in answer A) is briefly mentioned, this passage does not cover the history of the area sufficiently to be included in a history book. Answer C, a political treatise, is incorrect because the passage mentions nothing political at all. Answer D is incorrect because a travel brochure probably would give specific information on tourist sites and

accommodations. Answer E is not even logical; little sociological discussion was given in the passage.

3. **(C)** This is a detail or specific fact question. In the last sentence of the first paragraph you are told that Mount Klyuchevskaya is Siberia's highest point. Note that for this type of question, you should go back to the passage to find the right answer. Do not trust yourself to remember the fact; reskim the passage to assure yourself of getting the answer correct.

4. **(D)** The Ural Mountains are mentioned in the first paragraph. Since the word "mountains" is given in the plural, you may infer that there is more than one mountain and that the Urals are a mountain range. Answers B and C are rivers, not mountain ranges. Answer A may have tricked you. Mount Klyuchevskaya is *a* mountain; you may not assume it is a mountain range.

5. **(C)** The fourth paragraph mentions that there were three women who had won the Nobel Prize for Chemistry. Dr. Hodgkin won it in 1964, Marie Curie won it in 1911, and Irene Joliot-Curie won it in 1935. From these facts, you know that the first woman to win it was Marie Curie. If you chose answer D, you either misread the question or relied on your memory, remembering that Dr. Hodgkin had been awarded the prize. For a detail or specific fact question of this sort, go back to the passage and find the answer.

6. **(A)** Dr. Sabin is discussed in the second paragraph of the passage. There you are told that she was one of the first scientists to be concerned with the prevention of disease, rather than just its cure. Note that this is a rather tricky question because all of the answers given were mentioned somewhere in the passage. Again, you should have taken the time to go back and find the specific answer in the passage. If you had written a brief note in the margin next to each paragraph telling *which* doctor that paragraph discussed, you would have been able to save time by finding the right paragraph immediately.

7. **(C)** The passage simply narrates information. There is no particular emotion involved. For a question of this sort, you do not

go back to the passage. The answer will not be found there. You must infer the answer.

8. **(E)** The fourth paragraph tells you that Dr. Hodgkin was a crystallographer who won the Nobel Prize for Chemistry. However, it never defines the term "crystallographer." This type of question may be included to make you waste your time trying to find an answer. Go back and look, certainly, but if you cannot find a precise definition in just a few seconds, choose the answer that says the information was not given, and go on to the next question.

9. **(C)** The last sentence of the second paragraph states that a teacher may be forbidden by law to strike even a mild blow in exasperation. This is the only example given in the passage as a reason why the teacher might strike a child.

10. **(A)** This is the type of question where you had to think about your answer and ascribe a motive to the writer. You should *not* have gone back to the passage to look for an answer; one was not given there. Rarely will a passage directly state what an author's purpose is for writing a passage or making a specific statement. The author talks about robots after lamenting all the way through the passage that soon all human contact between students and teachers will be proscribed. You may therefore assume that robots are introduced to make the point that soon teachers will be no more than robots themselves.

NUMBER RIGHT:____(Give yourself one point for each.)

NUMBER WRONG:____(Multiply by ¼ point each.)

FINAL SCORE:____(Subtract the second number from the first; you may have an answer with a fraction, such as 16½.)

3.

DAY THREE

Hours One and Two: Math Review

Set Your Clock. *Today's study is unusual in that no new question types are being introduced. Instead, you are going to learn basic mathematical concepts and rules which may be tested on the SAT. Of course, you cannot learn everything about mathematics, algebra, geometry, and other quantitative fields in just a two-hour period. Therefore, this section introduces you to those subjects that are tested repeatedly, and refreshes your memory on those concepts which you might have forgotten (such as certain units of measurement).*

How to Learn This Material

You probably will have learned the rules given in this section sometime during your high school or college days; however, you may have forgotten "exact" formulas or the precise way to set up an equation. The following steps will help you *memorize* such information so that you will have it fresh in your mind the day of the exam. Try the following steps to achieve the best results in the least time.

1. *Read all the information.* Before you try to begin memorizing the material, you should read *all* of it at least once. You may be surprised at how much material you retain even from one quick reading.

2. *Organize the information.* This means that you categorize the information given in terms of your personal knowledge of that material. In other words, try to distinguish those rules with which you are very familiar (perhaps you just finished a class in geometry, and you know all the geometric rules and formulas), from those rules which you once knew but are now uncertain of (such

as algebra which you studied two years ago and haven't thought about since!). Once you have the material organized and categorized, you know which rules you may skim briefly, and which ones you should take the time to review very carefully.

3. *Make flash cards of the difficult concepts.* If you find that you are seeing material that is either new or very difficult for you, merely reading it will not be suficient. Trying to memorize rules which are lost among many others on a printed page may be difficult as well. Try *rewriting the rules on flash cards.* Take index cards and write the rules and formulas on them. You may wish to make up your own supplementary examples to help you recall the rules.

4. *Have a friend test you.* Ask a friend to use the flash cards to test your knowledge. After you feel you have mastered the information on your cards, you may still have time to have that friend test you on the other, less difficult, concepts. The more you review this material, the quicker you will be able to determine which rule to use on the exam and the easier you will find it to solve the problem.

5. *Review the material during your next day's lesson.* In your next study session, you will be learning about the two types of math questions you will encounter on the SAT. You will also be solving some practice problems. As you do each problem, stop and make a note of which formula or rule you used to solve that problem. Refer to these rules often to reinforce them in your mind.

The Rules

There are several basic concepts tested on the quantitative portion of the SAT. These concepts are introduced below, with critical formulas, rules, and vocabulary given.

Number Sets

Prime numbers: Prime numbers are integers which can be evenly divided only by themselves and 1. Examples: 2, 3, 5, 7, 11, 13, 17, 19, 23, 29.

Composite numbers: Composite numbers are the opposite of prime numbers. Composite numbers can be divided without a remainder by numbers other than themselves and 1. Examples: 4, 6, 8, 9, 12, 14, 15, 16, 18, 20.

NOTE: Do not confuse prime and composite numbers with odd and even numbers. While most prime numbers are odd (3, 5, 7, 9), one is even: 2. Composite numbers may be even (4, 6, 8) or odd (9, 15).

Whole numbers: A whole number is 0 or any positive multiple of 1. Whole numbers are usually defined as (0, 1, 2, 3 . . .) with the "..." meaning the set continues.

Integers: Integers are 0 and any positive (such as 2, 3) and negative (such as −2 or −3) whole numbers, as distinguished from fractions. Integers are usually defined as (. . . −3, −2, −1, 0, 1, 2, 3 . . .) with the "..." meaning the set continues in either direction.

- Integers include the set of whole numbers.

Rational numbers: Rational numbers are any numbers expressible as the quotient of two integers. Rational numbers are usually defined as a/b, where a and b are integers.

- Rational numbers include the sets of integers and whole numbers.

Irrational numbers: Irrational numbers are not capable of being expressed as the quotient of two integers. Rational numbers are usually defined as $\neq a/b$.

- Irrational numbers do *not* include rational numbers, integers, or whole numbers. Pi (π) is an example of an irrational number.

Real numbers: Real numbers are all of the above terms, including whole numbers, integers, rational numbers, and irrational numbers.

Units of Measurement

LINEAR MEASUREMENTS

12 inches = 1 foot
36 inches = 1 yard
3 feet = 1 yard
5,280 feet = 1 mile
1,760 yards = 1 mile

- Metric units are *not* tested on the SAT. You are *not* required to be able to convert inches to centimeters, or yards to meters. If metric terms are used at all, they will be predefined for you.

AREA MEASUREMENTS

144 square inches = 1 square foot (12″ × 12″)
9 square feet = 1 square yard (3′ × 3′)

- You should not bother to memorize the square inches in a square yard, the square feet in a square mile, or the square yards in a square mile. Those numbers are too large to be tested; if they should appear, you may calculate them by squaring the linear measurements. For example, since there are 1,760 yards in a mile, there are (1,760 × 1,760) square yards in a square mile. It is highly unlikely this will be tested.

- NOTE: *All area measurements are in square units.*

VOLUME MEASUREMENTS

You may find volume measurements by cubing a number. For example, since there are 3 feet in a yard, there are (3′ × 3′ × 3′=) 27 cubic feet in a cubic yard. Do not bother memorizing all the cubic measurements; they may be calculated quickly if necessary.

LIQUID OR OTHER VOLUME MEASUREMENTS

2 cups = 1 pint
2 pints = 1 quart
2 quarts = 1 half gallon
2 half gallons = 1 gallon

16 cups = 1 gallon
8 pints = 1 gallon
4 quarts = 1 gallon
2 half gallons = 1 gallon

• NOTE AGAIN: You are not expected to be able to convert quarts to liters.

TIME MEASUREMENTS

60 seconds = 1 minute
60 minutes = 1 hour
24 hours = 1 day
7 days = 1 week
52 weeks = 1 year
365 days = 1 year
366 days = 1 leap year

MONTHS

January:	31 days
February:	28 days
(29 days in a leap year)	
March:	31 days
April:	30 days
May:	31 days
June:	30 days
July:	31 days
August:	31 days
September:	30 days
October:	31 days
November:	30 days
December:	31 days

- You may have learned the "Days Rhyme" in elementary school. It is useful in helping to remember how many days are in which months. It goes:

> Thirty days has September,
> April, June, and November.
> All the rest have thirty-one
> But Feb. has twenty-eight for fun!

Algebra

The word "algebra" is derived from the Arabic term "al-jabr," meaning the reunion of broken parts. Algebra is a mathematical system used to generalize mathematical operations by using variables. Variables are letters that represent values. Typical variables are X, Y, Z or A, B, C.

When you see an algebra problem, you are usually asked to find the value of the variable. The question might say, "Solve for X." To do so, you must get the variable, the X, on one side of the equation and everything else on the other side.

If your equation is $3X + 3 = 9X - 3$, the similar terms are the $3X$ and $9X$ and the $+3$ and the -3. To combine terms, you must get them on the same side of the equal sign. Move the -3 to the left. It now becomes $+3$, since any number moved from one side to the other changes its sign. (If it were $+$ before, it is now $-$. If it were $-$ before, it is now $+$.) Next, move the $3X$ to the right, making it $-3X$. Your equation is now $3 + 3 = 9X - 3X$ (If there is no $+$ or $-$ in front of a number, you assume it is positive.) *Combine* like terms. Add the $3 + 3$ to get 6. Subtract $9X - 3X$ to get $6X$. You now have $6 = 6X$.

The final step is to divide *both* sides through by what is in front of the variable. You do this because you want to have the variable all by itself. Since a 6 is in front of the variable, divide both sides by a 6 to get

$$6/6 = 6X/6$$
$$1 = 1X; \ X = 1$$

Try another problem without the wordy explanation.

$$15 - 5X = 10X - 30$$
$$15 + 30 = 10X + 5X$$
$$45 = 15X$$
$$3 = X$$

This is the basic, simple type of algebra problem you will encounter. However, you may also have to multiply out variables such as

$$(a + b) (a + b).$$

You perform this multiplication one step at a time. Take the *a* in the first group and multiply it by the *a* in the second group to get a^2. Then take that same *a* in the first group and multiply it by the *b* in the second group to get *ab*.

Next, take the *b* in the first group and multiply it by the *a* in the second group to get *ba*. Take the *b* in the first group and multiply it by the *b* in the second group to get b^2.

You now have $a^2 + ab + ba + b^2$. The two central terms, *ab* and *ba*, are the same (when you multiply two numbers, you may do so in any order, such as 5×4 or 4×5). Combine terms to get $a^2 + 2ab + b^2$.

Try another problem without all the words:

$$(a - b) (a + b)$$
$$a \times a = a^2$$
$$a \times b = ab$$
$$-b \times a = -ab$$
$$-b \times b = -b^2$$
$$a^2 + ab - ab - b^2 = a^2 - b^2$$

(the +*ab* and the −*ab* cancel each other out).

While there are many other uses for algebra, if you have mastered these two concepts, you can do most of what you will find on the SAT. Again, you should be able to solve for a variable (Find X) and multiply variables together ["$(a + b) (a - b)$"].

Geometry

Closed Figures: Circles

The *midpoint* of a circle is a point in the center of the circle; the circle is usually named by its midpoint.

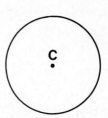

The *radius* of a circle is a line going from the midpoint of the circle to a point on the circumference of the circle.

The *diameter* of a circle is a straight line going from one side of a circle to the other, through the midpoint. A *diameter* is the same as two *radii*.

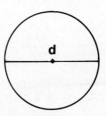

A *chord* is a line connecting *any* two points on a circle. The longest *chord* is the *diameter*; there are many other chords besides the *diameter*.

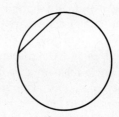

The *circumference* of a circle is its perimeter or outside line. The *circumfer-*

ence is found using the formula $C = 2\pi r$ where r is the radius. Since $2r$ is the same as $1d$ (diameter), you may also use the formula $C = \pi d$. Circumference is always in linear units.

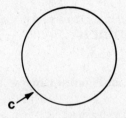

The interior angle measure of *any* circle is 360°.

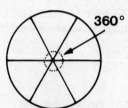

The *area* of a circle is found using the formula $A = \pi r^2$, where r is the radius. The *area* of a circle is always in square units.

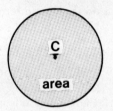

An *arc* is a part of a circle's circumference. You find it using the following formula: Fraction (that the central angle is of the total number of degrees in the circle) times circumference. In the example below, XY is the *arc*. The central angle XCY measures 60°. The total angle measure of a circle is 360°; 60° is 1/6 of 360°. Therefore, the *arc* is 1/6 of the circle's circumference. Find the circumference ($C = 2\pi r$; here that is 6π). $1/6 \times 6\pi = 1\pi$.

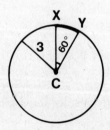

A *sector* is a part of a circle's area. You find it using the following formula: Fraction (that the central angle is of the total number of degrees in the circle) times area. In the example below, XCY is the *sector*. The central angle XCY measures 120°. The total angle measure of a circle is 360°; 120° is ⅓ of that. Therefore, the *sector* is ⅓ of the circle's area. Find the area ($A = \pi r^2$; here that is 36π). ⅓ × 36π = 12π.

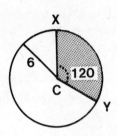

Closed Figures

Polygons are closed figures that lie in one plane. The name of a polygon is determined by its number of sides and interior angles.

Triangle	3 sides/angles	Heptagon	7 sides/angles
Quadrilateral	4 sides/angles	Octagon	8 sides/angles
Pentagon	5 sides/angles	Nonagon	9 sides/angles
Hexagon	6 sides/angles	Decagon	10 sides/angles

The *exterior* angle measure of any polygon is 360°.

The *interior* angle measure of any polygon may be found using the following formula: $(S - 2)$ $(180°)$ where S stands for the number of sides the figure has. When 2 is subtracted from the number of sides of a figure, the resulting number is the number of triangles into which the figure may be divided. Each triangle has an interior angle measure of 180°. Multiplying the number of triangles $(S - 2)$ by the interior angle measure of each triangle $(180°)$ gives the interior angle measure of the whole polygon.

The *average* measure of one angle of a polygon may be found using the following formula: $\frac{(S-2)(180°)}{S}$.

Find the total degrees in the interior of the figure; divide it by the number of angles. The number of interior angles is the same as the number of sides, S.

A *regular* polygon has *equal* sides and *equal* angles. Any angle in a regular polygon may be found using the formula $\frac{(S-2)(180°)}{S}$ since all angles are equal.

Triangles are polygons with three sides. There are three types of triangles: *scalene* (with no equal sides and no equal angles); *isosceles* (with two equal sides and two equal angles); and *equilateral* (with three equal sides and three equal angles). An *equilateral* triangle is a *regular polygon* (since all of its sides and angles are equal).

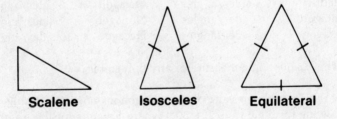

Scalene   **Isosceles**   **Equilateral**

The interior angles of any triangle add up to 180°. The interior angles of any *quadrilateral* add up to 360° (since a quadrilateral may be divided into two triangles, as shown in the figure).

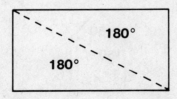

The area of a triangle is found using the formula: ½ *bh*, where *b* is the base and *h* is the height.

The area of a quadrilateral is found using the formula: *bh*, where *b* is the base and *h* is the height. NOTE: With some quadrilaterals, the letters change but the concept is the same. For example, the area of a rectangle is *lw*, where *l* is the length and *w* is the width. This is the same as *bh* because the base is the same as the length and the height is the same as the width. The area of a square is s^2, where *s* stands for side. This is the same as base times height as well, because all sides of a square are equal.

The area of a *trapezoid* is ½(b_1 + b_2)*h* where b_1 stands for one base, b_2 stands for the other, and *h* stands for the height. Since in a *trapezoid*, opposite bases are parallel but not necessarily equal, the average length of the bases must be found.

Simple Angles

An angle measuring less than 90° is called *acute*.

An angle measuring exactly 90° is called *right*. It is often indicated by a small box in the angle.

An angle measuring more than 90° but less than 180° is called *obtuse*.

An angle measuring exactly 180° is called *straight*. Angles along a straight line must add up to 180°.

An angle measuring more than 180° but less than 360° is called *reflexive*.

Angles that add up to 90° are called *complementary*.

Angles that add up to 180° are called *supplementary*.

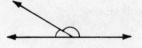

Angles that are opposite one another are called *vertical* angles. Vertical angles are equal.

Around two parallel lines crossed by a transversal, all acute angles are equal and all obtuse angles are equal. (If you have difficulty determining which angles are acute and which are obtuse, you might note that all angles *in the same position* are equal. Angles 1 and 5 in the figure are both in the upper left corner and are equal.)

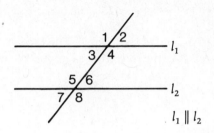

Fractions and Decimals

All fractions may be converted to decimals and percentages. You should *memorize* the following most common fractions for use on the exam.

½ = .50 = 50%	⅙ ~ $.\overline{166}$ = 16⅔%	⅛ = .125 = 12.5%
⅓ ~ $.\overline{33}$ = 33⅓%	⅚ ~ .83 = 83⅓%	⅜ = .375 = 37.5%
⅔ ~ $.\overline{66}$ = 66⅔%	1/7 ~ .14 ~ 14%	⅝ = .625 = 62.5%
¼ = .25 = 25%	2/7 ~ .29 ~ 29%	⅞ = .875 = 87.5%
¾ = .75 = 75%	3/7 ~ .43 ~ 43%	1/9 ~ $.\overline{11}$ ~ 11%
⅕ = .20 = 20%	4/7 ~ .57 ~ 57%	2/9 ~ $.\overline{22}$ ~ 22%
⅖ = .40 = 40%	5/7 ~ .71 ~ 71%	4/9 ~ $.\overline{44}$ ~ 44%
⅗ = .60 = 60%	6/7 ~ .86 ~ 86%	5/9 ~ .56 ~ 56%
⅘ = .80 = 80%		7/9 ~ $.\overline{77}$ ~ 78%
		8/9 ~ $.\overline{88}$ ~ 89%

If you forget a fraction/decimal equivalency, you may find it mathematically by dividing the bottom number into the top.

Fractions and decimals become *larger* when *added* but *smaller* when *multiplied*. ⅓ + ⅓ = ⅔, ⅓ × ⅓ = 1/9

Fractions and decimals become *smaller* when subtracted but *larger* when *divided*. $\frac{2}{3} - \frac{1}{3} = \frac{1}{3}$, $\frac{2}{3} \div \frac{1}{3} = \left(\frac{\frac{2}{3}}{\frac{1}{3}} \cdot \frac{\frac{3}{1}}{\frac{3}{1}} = \frac{\frac{6}{3}}{1} = \right) 2$

A decimal may be converted to a percent by moving the decimal point two places to the right. .625 = 62.5%.

A fraction is a part divided by a whole. The formula is sometimes expressed as *is/of*, as in the following example: What fraction *of* 50 is 25? $\frac{25}{50} = \frac{1}{2}$.

Ratios

A *ratio* may be found using the formula *of/to*. Example: What is the ratio *of* 8 dogs *to* 2 cats? 8/2 = 4/1 or 4:1.

To use a ratio to find a *total*, *add* the numbers in the ratio. The total must be a *multiple* of that sum. Example: With a ratio of 8 dogs to 2 cats, the total must be (8 + 2 = 10) a multiple of 10. There may be 10, 20, 30, 40, etc., dogs and cats. There could not be 11, 22, 33, etc.

To use a ratio and a partial total to find a specific number, look for the *number of sets*. Example: If there is a ratio of 8 dogs to 2 cats, and there are 16 dogs, how many cats are there? Since 16 is *two sets* of 8, there must also be *two sets* of 2, or 4 cats. If there is a ratio of 6 dogs to 7 cats, and there are 35 cats, how many dogs are there? Since 35 is *five sets* of 7, there must also be *five sets* of 6, or 30 dogs.

Graphs

With *any* graph, you should take the following approach:

1. *Read the title to determine what is being graphically represented.* The title will tell you what information you are being given. Trick questions may trap you if you don't read the title carefully. For example, if the title is "Number of Men in San Francisco in 1985,"

you *cannot* answer a question on the *number of people* in San Francisco in 1985. The graph only tells you how many *men* there are, not how many *women*. You *cannot* assume that men are 50% of the population. You also could not answer a question on the number of men in San Jose (rather than San Francisco), or the number of men in San Francisco in 1984 (rather than 1985).

2. *Read the axes to determine your units.* There are usually two axes, one vertical and one horizontal. Each will be labeled; read the label to determine whether you are talking about tens, hundreds, or thousands, or whether you are talking about days, weeks, or months. If you don't read the axes, you may be tricked by a question that wants an answer in days. If the graph gives the information in weeks only, you would have to multiply the number of weeks by seven (since there are seven days in a week).

3. *Read the key to determine what the artwork means.* You will have, usually to the right of the graph, a box or figure showing that the shaded portion represents one thing, the white portion represents another thing, and the polka dots or stripes represent a third thing. Take the time to read this key carefully. If the polka dots represent the number of *women*, you *cannot* answer a question on the number of *girls* since *girls* and *women* are two different categories. If the key tells you that the stripes represent the number of *tenured teachers*, you cannot answer a question on the number of *teachers*, since you may not assume all teachers are tenured.

4. *Read any notes.* Often below the figure there will be a small note, telling you that the school year goes from September to June (as opposed to a regular 12-month year); this information could be very important should you later have to divide a total by a number of months. You may be told that the total is a certain number; this information could be critical should you have to find an exact number using a percentage graph.

4.

DAY FOUR

Hour One: Quantitative Comparisons

Set Your Clock. *You will have a full hour to review the first of two types of mathematics questions you will find on the SAT. The quantitative comparisons are quite different from most math questions you have had on standardized exams or school tests over the years. Please take the time, therefore, to go through this section especially carefully. Because the questions in this section are so unusual, you want to make certain that you understand their format precisely before going on to the actual exam.*

Question Style

Each quantitative comparison consists of information given in two columns. At the top of the page will be the titles Column A and Column B. Information will be printed in both columns for each question. Such information may be a phrase, a word, numerals, or symbols.

EXAMPLE:	COLUMN A	COLUMN B
	The cost of 10 cars at $8,000 each	The cost of 8 cars at $10,000 each

EXAMPLE:	$\sqrt{36}$	6^2

If information is to be used in both columns, that information is centered between the two columns.

EXAMPLE:

$$X < 0$$

X^2 X^3

A variable (a letter such as X or Y or A or B) or a symbol (such as # or *) represents the same number or operation throughout the problem.

EXAMPLE: $(X + 4)^2 - 3$ $(X - 3)^2 - 4$

NOTE: Do not solve for X in one problem and then assume that X retains that value into the next question. For example, in one question, X may equal 3, while in the next question X may equal 1/5 and in the third question may equal 0.

Any diagrams or figures will *not necessarily* be drawn to scale. This means that you are not able simply to look at a problem and use your eyes to determine angle measurements or sizes. For example, in the figure below, you cannot automatically assume that angle X is larger than angle Y.

Summary. Your problems are not actually "questions" in the strictest sense of the word. Rarely will you see a complete statement, such as "What is the value of X?" Instead, you will simply see "X."

The Answer Choices

This unusual question type has *four* possible answers. *Note that this is the only portion of the exam where there are only four possible answers rather than five.* You have answer choices A, B, C, and D, as opposed to your standard choices A, B, C, D, and E. If you guess an answer, never fill in an E; you will of course have no chance of guessing the correct answer by doing so.

Quantitative comparisons require you to compare quantities. You will see two quantities, one in Column A and one in Column B. You are to compare them and determine whether one is larger, whether they are equal, or whether you cannot make the comparison.

If the quantity in Column A is larger than the quantity in Column B, your answer is A.

EXAMPLE: **COLUMN A** **COLUMN B**

⅙ 16%

In this example, the quantity in Column A is larger than the quantity in Column B. You might have been tempted to say they are equal, but 1/6 is actually 16.66%, a number slightly larger than 16%. This type of question is common. It takes only a second to answer, but you have to be very careful not to be too complacent, to fall into the trap of automatically assuming that two similar-appearing quantities are exactly equal.

If the quantity in Column B is larger than the quantity in Column A, your answer is B.

EXAMPLE: **COLUMN A** **COLUMN B**

33% ⅓

In this example, the quantity in Column B is larger than the quantity in Column A. The fraction ⅓ is actually 33 ⅓%, which is larger than 33%. Again, this is a simple, quickly answered question—if you are careful.

If the quantity in Column A is equal to the quantity in Column B, your answer is C.

EXAMPLE: **COLUMN A** **COLUMN B**

⅗ 60%

Because 3/5 is *exactly* equal to 60%, the quantities are equal. If, for some reason, you have not memorized all of the fraction/percentage equivalencies, you could quickly solve this problem by dividing 3 by 5. Your answer is exactly .6, which is the same as 60%.

If you *cannot* make a comparison between the quantities in the two columns, your answer is D.

EXAMPLE: COLUMN A   COLUMN B

              The number of   30
              days in a month

You do not have enough information to compare the quantities. To find the number in Column A, you have to know *which* month you are considering: February (with 28, or even 29 in a leap year), March with 31, or April with 30? Without the information, you cannot compare the quantities. NOTE: Even if Column A had been 30 and Column B had had the statement, the answer would still be D. It makes no difference whether you cannot find an answer for Column A, for Column B, or for both columns.

Review

   A = Column A is larger
   B = Column B is larger
   C = Both columns are equal
   D = The columns can't be compared

Directions

The math section is preceded by rather lengthy directions. If you see and understand them now, you will not need to spend time reading and trying to comprehend them when you take the actual exam.

· The directions begin by stating that "all numbers used are real numbers." You learned in yesterday's lesson that the set of real numbers includes all whole numbers, integers, rational numbers, and irrational numbers. In general, the set of real numbers includes everything you have ever worked with. There are numbers called imaginary numbers; they are much too sophisticated to be tested on this exam. Don't be concerned, therefore, with this direction.

The second direction is a set of statements regarding any figures drawn on the exam. Let's go through each of these in detail.

First, you are told that you may assume as correct the positions of points, angles, and regions. This means that if on a number line, *X* is to the right of *Y*, *X* is larger than *Y*.

EXAMPLE:

Here, *Y* is negative (since it is to the left of 0) and *X* is positive (since it is to the right of 0). Any positive number is greater than any negative number.

Second, you are told that angle measures are positive. This means that there are no angles that measure 0° or negative numbers, such as −60° or −90°.

Third, you are told that "you may assume that lines that appear to be straight are straight." This simply means that no one is trying to trick you with lines that are slightly bent or curved.

Fourth, you are told that "unless otherwise indicated, figures lie in a plane." This statement is for those persons who have had a lot of upper level geometry. It simply means that standard, beginning geometry is all you need to know to do any problems on this exam.

Finally, you are told that "unless you are told a figure is drawn to scale, you may not assume it is so." This is similar to what you heard before. In other words, you cannot trust your eyes to tell you that one angle is larger than another, or that a particular angle is a right (90°) angle.

After you go through all the directions on the figures, you are given your "standard directions." These tell you that you will see two quantities which are to be compared, and that you should choose A if the quantity in Column A is larger, B if the quantity in Column B is larger, C if both quantities are equal, and D if you cannot compare the quantities. These answer choices were discussed in greater detail earlier in this material.

After the directions is a brief note reminding you never to choose E. *Please remember this:* If you find that you have only one minute left, but you have several problems incomplete, you *may* want to fill in some ovals to take a chance on getting some answers correct. However, be certain not to fill in oval E and waste your guess.

Lastly, you are told that common information (information to be used in one or both of the columns) is centered between the columns.

An example will be given at the end of these directions. It is generally a very, very simplistic one, such as the difference between adding 1 to 1 and subtracting 1 from 1.

Summary. The directions take up about ¾ of a column and can look very intimidating. If you understand the brief analysis given above, you can skim them or skip them entirely and go right to the problems.

How to Do the Problems

Since you are only comparing quantities, not looking for a final, precise answer, you want to avoid doing any more calculating than absolutely necessary. The following steps will help you make the best use of your time.

1. *Read both columns.* Take the time to read any information centered between the columns, then read Column A *and* Column B. Do *not* fall into the trap of beginning to calculate an answer for Column A before you read Column B. Chances are you will not have to do any calculations at all.

EXAMPLE: COLUMN A   COLUMN B

356 × 234   65 × 0 × 1,281

Had you read only Column A, you might have wasted your time actually multiplying out these numbers. However, had you done the smart thing and looked at Column B, you would have noted that one of the numbers to be multiplied is a 0. Since *any number or numbers* multiplied by a 0 must equal 0, you automatically know that Column B is 0. Since both numbers in Column A are positive, you know that the product of those numbers must be positive. *Any* positive number is greater than 0; therefore, *regardless of the actual value* in Column A, Column A is greater than Column B. Choose answer A.

2.   *Look at your operations.* Operations are what you do to the numbers, such as addition, subtraction, multiplication, and division. Often you will find that the operation makes a difference in the answer, so that you don't have to work out the entire problem.

EXAMPLE: COLUMN A   COLUMN B

½ + ¼   ½ × ¼

When you add fractions, they become *larger*. When you multiply fractions, they become *smaller*. Since the fractions are the same in both columns, and Column A becomes larger while Column B becomes smaller, you know that Column B must be smaller than Column A. Choose answer A.

3.   *Look for equal proportions.* You may find that the two columns are saying the same thing in two different ways. For example, multiplication is commutative, which means that it may be done in any order. $5 \times 4 = 4 \times 5$. If Column A said 456×890 and Column B said 890×456, you would know to choose answer C since both columns have equal quantities being multiplied. Often this same principle is tested in a slightly more sophisticated way.

EXAMPLE: COLUMN A   COLUMN B

300% of   200% of 75
200% of
25

In Column A, 300% of 200% is the same as 3 times and 2 times, or 6 times 25. In Column B, 200% is the same as 2 times. Since 25 is ⅓ of 75, and you are multiplying it 3 times as often as you are multiplying 75, the columns are equal (6 × 25 = 150; 2 × 75 = 150). Choose answer C.

4. *Solve the problem.* If all else fails and you cannot find any short cuts or tricks, go ahead and work the problem through. Usually there will be some short cut; however, don't spend so much time looking for it that you defeat your own purpose. If you do work through the problem, try to stop as soon as possible. In other words, don't do each and every calculation out to its final steps. If you see that Column A is going to have 65 × 48 while Column B is going to have 68 × 49, you know that Column B is going to be larger (since each number to be multiplied in Column B is larger than each number to be multiplied in Column A).

EXAMPLE   COLUMN A   COLUMN B

          −465 × 36   21 × −797

In this instance, there are no obvious short cuts. Each column has one negative and one positive. Each column uses multiplication; therefore, each answer will be negative. When you multiply Column A out, you get −16,740. Column B's product is −16,737. As you see, the answers are so close that estimation would be difficult.

NOTE: When you do notice that you have to work out a problem of this sort, decide whether doing so is worth your time. You may find that you can go through five or six other problems using short cuts in the time it would take you to work all the way through this one problem.

Traps to Avoid

When *reading* the quantitative comparison questions, you should be careful to avoid the following traps:

1. *Do not carry over information from one problem to another.* If you just found out that "X = 15" in one problem don't assume that it

has the same value in another problem. It is very easy to do so; watch yourself carefully.

2. *Don't misread the operation signs.* Many problems have been missed because a student saw that the numbers in Column A were separated by plus signs and just automatically assumed that the numbers in Column B were as well. Perhaps Column A called for addition while Column B called for subtraction. Look at the signs in *both* columns.

3. *Don't gloss over the additional information that is centered between the columns.* Often such information gives *vital* facts, such as whether a number is positive ($X>0$) or negative ($X<0$).

When *solving* the quantitative comparison questions, you should be careful to avoid the following traps.

1. *Don't make rough estimates unless you know that the quantities are so far apart that doing so is expected.* In other words, with a problem like the one given earlier (where Column A came out to be −16,740 and Column B came out to be −16,737), making an estimate would possibly cause you to miss the problem. Look carefully before you estimate.

2. *Keep your calculations neat.* This may sound elementary, but doing sloppy calculations has led to many a missed problem. If you don't keep track of your positive and negative signs and make certain your decimal point is properly positioned, you could easily miss a question that should be very basic.

3. *Do not choose answer E under any circumstances.*

Time-saving Suggestions

1. *Estimate whenever feasible.* Often, you will find that you can make a very rough estimate, or simply determine that one column will be positive while the other will be negative or zero. Don't do any specific calculations unless absolutely necessary.

2. *Skip around within the section.* As long as you keep track of your numbering, you should feel free to skip problems you find trou-

blesome. If you don't understand a problem, or have no idea how to begin working it, choose any answer at random and fill in your answer grid. Place an arrow next to the problem in your test booklet (don't make stray marks on your answer grid) so that you can go back to it if you have a chance. If you understand a problem only too well, and know that you could do it but it would take you some time for lengthy calculations, you may also wish to skip the problem and return to it later.

3. *Use the information given.* Often, one column (usually Column B) will have a specific number. Work backwards, using it to help you with Column A. For example, if Column A is 5026/13 and Column B is 386, just multiply 386 by 13 and see what you get. You will get, in this instance, 5018, telling you that 5026/13 must be larger than 386. If you worked the problem all the way through, you would find that 5026/13 = 386.61538. Most people find that multiplying numbers is easier than dividing them. Use the numbers given and work with them.

Practice Exam: Quantitative Comparisons

Please take the following practice exam on quantitative comparisons. The portion of the SAT that has both quantitative comparison and problem solving questions generally features 20 QC questions; therefore, that is the number of questions you are given in this practice exam. An answer key and explanatory answers follow. Score yourself and remember: incorrect answers on this portion cost you ⅓ point each (on all other portions of the exam, incorrect answers cost you only ¼ point each).

NOTE: On the actual exam, you are likely to see three examples following the directions, preceding the problems. In the interests of time and space, only one example is given in this exam.

Quantitative Comparisons

General Information

All numbers used are real numbers.

You may assume as correct the positions of points, angles, and regions.

Angle measures are positive.

You may assume that lines that appear to be straight are straight.

Unless otherwise indicated, figures lie in a plane.

Unless you are told a figure is drawn to scale, you may not assume it is so.

DIRECTIONS: Compare the quantity in Column A with the quantity in Column B and choose answer

A if the quantity in Column A is larger
B if the quantity in Column B is larger
C if both quantities are equal
D if you cannot determine the relationship between the quantities

Write in your answer choice next to each question number.

There is no answer choice E.

Information regarding one or both of the quantities is given centered between the columns.

EXAMPLE:	COLUMN A	COLUMN B
A	$1 + 1$	$1 - 1$
1.	Average of 5, 7, 9, 11, 13	Average of 7, 8, 9, 10, 11
2.	Area of a circle whose longest chord is 4	Area of a circle of radius 2

3.
$$3Y = 6X$$

X 1

4.

Area of *AEC*   50% of the area of *ABCD*

5.
$$\text{Set } Z = (2, 3, 4, 5, 6, 7)$$

Number of prime numbers in Set Z   Number of composite numbers in Set Z

6.
$$X^2 = Y$$

X Y

7.   The dress sold for 125% of its original cost

Profit $25.00

8.   The average weight of three men is 150 lb.

Total weight of the men   400 lb

9.

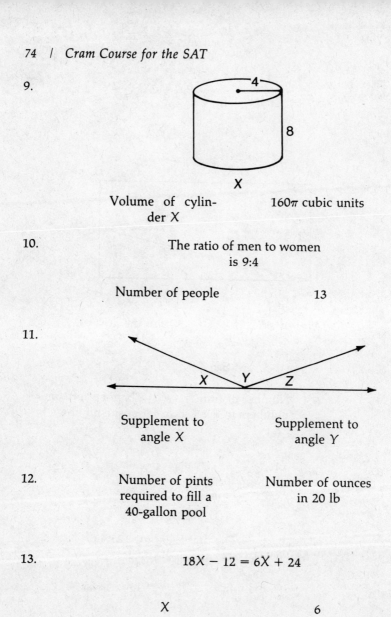

| Volume of cylinder X | 160π cubic units |

10.

| The ratio of men to women is 9:4 | |
| Number of people | 13 |

11.

| Supplement to angle X | Supplement to angle Y |

12.

| Number of pints required to fill a 40-gallon pool | Number of ounces in 20 lb |

13.

$$18X - 12 = 6X + 24$$

| X | 6 |

14.

| a, b are positive | |
| $(a - b)^2$ | $(a + b)^2$ |

15.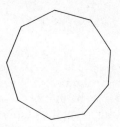

Number of de-
grees in interior
angles of the
figure

1300

16. $\dfrac{\dfrac{1}{6}}{7}$

116%

17. $A * B = \dfrac{½ (A - B)}{B}$

.5

8 * 4

18. Last year Rufus sold 12 dozen
eggs. This year he sold 168 eggs.

Percent of increase in
number of eggs sold

⅙

19. Area of a hexagon with
total interior angle
measure of 720°

Area of a heptagon with
total interior angle
measure of 900°

20. $6ab$

$(3a)(2b)$

ANSWER KEY

1. C	6. D	11. D	16. A
2. C	7. D	12. C	17. C
3. D	8. A	13. B	18. A
4. C	9. B	14. B	19. D
5. A	10. D	15. B	20. C

Explanations

1. **(C)** You *could* have wasted time doing this averaging problem "the old-fashioned way," adding all the numbers and dividing by the number of numbers. However, you should have noted that in Column A the numbers are evenly spaced (they are two units apart) such that the number in the middle is automatically the average: 9. In Column B, the numbers are consecutive (they come right after one another), such that the number in the middle is automatically the average: 9. Note that this type of problem should only have taken you a few seconds; the columns are equal. Choose answer C.

2. **(C)** In Column A, you have to know that the longest chord in a circle *is* the diameter. Therefore, Column A is really asking you what the area of a circle of diameter 4 is. Since the diameter is the same as two radii, you know that the radius of that circle is 2. *Do not bother finding the actual area.* Had you read *both* columns before doing any work, you would recognize that Column B asks for exactly the same thing: the area of a circle of radius 2. While finding the area with such a simple radius would not be difficult, you need not take even the few seconds required. Choose answer C.

3. **(D)** This question might have tricked you. If you put answer C, you were careless. Because $3Y = 6X$, it takes twice as many Xs to reach a quantity as it takes Ys. For example, if Y were 2, X would have to be 1. If Y were 4, X would be 2. However, you know only the proportion or ratio of Y to X. You don't know any exact numbers. X could be 1, in which case Y would be 2. Or X could be greater than 1 or less than 1. (Both X and Y could be 0.) You have insufficient information to solve for an actual value for X. Choose answer D.

4. **(C)** AEC is a triangle inscribed in the rectangle $ABCD$. Any triangle inscribed in a rectangle must have an area ½ that of the rectangle. The area of a triangle is ½ bh, one-half base times height. Here, the base is AC and the height is FE. (FE must be equal to AB and CD because it is parallel to those lines.) For the rectangle $ABCD$, the area is lw, length times width. The length is CD and the width is AC. Therefore, you

are using the same values to find the area of the rectangle as to find the area of the triangle. Since the triangle multiplies the values by ½, its area must be ½ that of the rectangle. Choose answer C.

5. **(A)** Prime numbers are those which may be evenly divided only by themselves and 1. The prime numbers in Set Z are 2, 3, 5, 7; there are four. Composite numbers are the opposite of prime numbers (any number that is not prime is composite). Composite numbers may be divided evenly by numbers other than just themselves and 1. The composite numbers in Set Z are 4 and 6; there are two. *Note the trap.* If you forgot that 2 is prime (it is, in fact, the only even prime), you might have chosen answer C, believing that there are three primes and three composites. Since 2 is prime, there are more primes than composites. Choose answer A.

6. **(D)** This was another difficult, tricky question. You might have automatically (and carelessly) thought that Y must be larger than X, because X had to be multiplied by itself to become as large as Y. However, don't forget that both numbers could be 0 or 1. This means that the variables *could* be equal or (if you used other values, such as 3 and 9), X could be smaller than Y. Since you could have two different situations, you cannot determine the relationship between the quantities. Choose answer D.

7. **(D)** The formula to be used in this type of problem is $S = C + P$, Sales price equals Cost plus Profit. In order to find out one specific number, you need at least one number to begin with. Here, you are given no specific number, just a percentage. You know that the profit was 25% of the original cost; however, you have no idea of the original cost. Therefore, you cannot assume that the original cost was $100, so that 25% of it would be $25. If the original cost were only $40, the profit would be a mere $10. If the original cost were $400, the profit would be $100. Without more information, you can't determine the relationship between the columns. Choose answer D.

8. **(A)** If three men averaged 150 lb each, their total weight must be 3 times that average, or $(150 \times 3 =)$ 450 lb. It makes no dif-

ference that you don't know exactly how much each man weighed; you are only asked to find the total weight. Even if one man weighed 100 lb, a second weighed 200 lb, and a third weighed 150 lb, the total is the same. If you chose answer D, assuming that you didn't have enough information to answer this question, you didn't think the question through. Since the three men total 450 lb, choose answer A.

9. **(B)** The volume of a figure is found by multiplying the area of the base times the height. With a cylinder, the base is a circle. The area of a circle is πr^2. Here, r is 4, so that $\pi r^2 = 16\pi$. Next, you would multiply 16 π by 8. However, you should not actually do this multiplication. When you look at Column B and see 160, you should know that is the larger number. You know that 16 times 10 would be 160; here you are multiplying 16 by a mere 8. Thus, your answer must be less than 160 and Column B must be larger. Choose answer B.

10. **(D)** Did this question trick you? If the ratio of men to women is 9:4, there are 9 men for every 4 women. Therefore, there could be a total of 13 people, 9 men and 4 women. Or, there could be 26 people, 18 men and 8 women. Or there could be 39 people, 27 men and 12 women. In other words, there could be any number of people, as long as the ratio of men to women remains 9:4. This means that there must be a total number of people that is a multiple of 13. There could not be, for example, 14 people, because there would be 9 men, 4 women—and one something or other left over! The total must always be a multiple of the sum of the numbers in the ratio, but it could be any multiple. Choose answer D.

11. **(D)** Angles X, Y, and Z are all along a straight line and thus are supplementary. Angles that are supplementary add up to 180°. The supplement to angle X is the sum of angles Y and Z. The supplement to angle Y is the sum of angles X and Z. Since Z remains constant, you are really comparing X to Y. Since you cannot assume the figure is drawn to scale, you cannot assume angles X and Y are equal. You don't have enough information to compare the quantities. Choose answer D.

12. **(C)** If you know your units of measurement (which you should have memorized), this is a simple problem. You should *not* have done any calculations at all. Since there are 8 pints to a gallon, there would be 8 × 40 pints in a 40-gallon pool. Since there are 16 ounces in a pound, there would be 16 × 20 ounces in 20 lb. Note the proportional relationship between the columns: 8 is ½ of 16; 40 is twice 20. Therefore, regardless of what the actual result is, the columns are equal. Try to look for these types of short cuts whenever possible. Choose answer C.

13. **(B)** This is a standard algebra problem. You must move the numbers to have all the X terms on one side and all the non-X terms on the other. Move the $6X$ to the left, making it $-6X$. Remember that when you move from one side of the equals sign to the other, you make a $(+)$ into a $(-)$ and a $(-)$ into a $(+)$. Move the -12 from the left to the right, making it $+12$. Now you have $18X - 6X = 24 + 12$. Combine like terms to get $12X = 36$. Divide both sides through by the 12 (so that you end up with just X on one side) to get $36/12 = 3$. $X = 3$. Choose answer B.

14. **(B)** The key to this problem is the information that a and b are *positive*. This means that they are not negative and they are not zero. In this case, adding a positive to a must make the quantity larger than subtracting that same number. NOTE: This problem was a commonsense one; you should not have bothered to write out all the terms. However, if you did not see the "point" of the question, you could have used another short cut.

    You should have *memorized* the fact that $(a - b)^2 = a^2 - 2ab + b^2$ and the fact that $(a + b) = a^2 + 2ab + b^2$. The a^2's and the b^2's are the same in both columns; only the $-2ab$ and the $+2ab$ are different. Since a and b are positive, you know that a $+2ab$ must be larger than a $-2ab$. Choose answer B.

15. **(B)** The figure is a nonagon (it has nine sides). To find the total interior degree measure, subtract 2 from the number of sides and multiply by $180°$. You should remember the formula $(S - 2)(180°)$ where S represents the number of sides. By

subtracting 2 from the number of sides, you find the number of triangles. Since each triangle contains 180°, multiply the number of triangles by 180°. Here, you have 7 × 180°. Unfortunately, the numbers are too close to estimate in this instance; you should (for a change) do the calculations. Seven times 180° = 1260°. Choose answer B.

16. **(A)** You have the number one (which is the same as the fraction $\frac{1}{1}$, since any number is the same as itself over one) divided by the fraction six-sevenths. When you divide by a fraction, you invert (turn the number upside down) and multiply. This gives you $\frac{1}{1} \times \frac{7}{6}$. Multiply the numerators to get (1 × 7 = 7) and the denominators to get (1 × 6 = 6) $\frac{7}{6}$. Since $\frac{7}{6}$ is $1\frac{1}{6}$, and $\frac{1}{6}$ is approximately equal to 16%, you might have thought the quantities were equal. However, $\frac{1}{6}$ is not equal to 16%; it is .166666 with the 6's repeating, such that $\frac{1}{6}$ is *greater* than 16% and $1\frac{1}{6}$ is *greater* than 116%. Choose answer A.

17. **(C)** This is a symbolism problem. Use the example, the common information, to determine what the symbol is telling you to do. Here you learn that the * means that when you have two numbers (*A* and *B* in this instance), you subtract the second from the first (*A* − *B*) then take ½ of that answer. Then you divide that by the second number. Here, the numbers are 8 and 4. First, subtract the second number from the first to get (8 − 4=) 4. Then take ½ of that to get (½ × 4=) 2. Now divide your answer of 2 by the second number to get ($\frac{2}{4}$=) $\frac{2}{4}$ or ½. Since ½ is the same as .5, choose answer C.

Note that in a symbolism problem like this, all you need to do is determine what the symbol is telling you to do, then do it one step at a time. In this instance, you substituted the 8 for the A and the 4 for the B, then performed the same operations with 8 and 4 as the example did with A and B.

18. **(A)** Since there are 12 to a dozen, if Rufus sold 12 dozen eggs, he sold (12 × 12 =) 144 eggs last year and 168 this year. To find the percentage increase in the number of eggs sold, find the number increase (168 − 144= 24 additional eggs) and put it over the original whole (the number of eggs sold last year, 144). $\frac{24}{144}$ = $\frac{1}{6}$. *Don't fall into the trap here!* There was a $\frac{1}{6}$ in-

crease, which is the same as (approximately) 16.6%, *not* ⅙%. If you chose answer C, saying the columns were equal, you were saying that there was *one-sixth of 1 percent* increase, when in fact there was a ⅙ or 16.6% increase. Choose answer A.

19. **(D)** The interior angle measure of a figure has nothing to do with its area. Any hexagon has an interior angle measure of 720°, since you find the measure with the formula $(S - 2)(180°)$, where S is the number of sides of the figure. Since a hexagon has 6 sides, you would have $(6 - 2)(180°)$, or $4 \times 180° = 720°$. This is true whether the hexagon is huge or miniscule. The same reasoning applies with a heptagon; it is a seven-sided figure that always has an interior angle measure of 900°, regardless of its size. Do not be tricked into choosing answer B simply because the total interior angle measure of one figure is larger than that of another figure; the more sides a figure has, the greater the total interior angle measure will be. The angle measure does not tell you the relative sizes of the figures. You do not have sufficient information to answer the question; choose answer D.

20. **(C)** This should have been a simple question. Since you have no idea of the values of a and b, you cannot "simplify" them in any way; you can only multiply them together to get ab. Multiply the numerals to get $(3 \times 2 =)6$; combine to get $6ab$.

NUMBER RIGHT:____(Give yourself one point for each.)

NUMBER WRONG:____(Multiply by ⅓ point each.)

FINAL SCORE:____(Subtract the second number from the first; you may have an answer with a fraction such as 14⅔.)

Hour Two: Problem Solving

Set Your Clock. *You should have used your first hour of this day's study time to learn about quantitative comparisons. This second hour will be devoted to the second type of mathematics question you will find on the SAT, the problem solving question. You will be glad to know that this type of question is much more familiar, and consequently much easier to understand, than the quantitative comparison question. Therefore, if you finish this section early, you may wish to spend your extra time going over the quantitative comparison material a second time.*

The Question Style

The problem solving question is the basic multiple choice mathematics question you have seen on standardized exams before. You are given a question to answer or a problem to solve. You will then be given five answer choices; you are to choose the correct one. There will be only one correct answer. Occasionally, a question asks you to find an approximate solution. In such an instance, choose the best answer, the one that is closest to the precise answer.

Most problem solving questions will be relatively short. Some will have additional information, in the form of a chart, graph, table, or figure, in the margin or above the problem. Some charts, graphs, tables, or figures are used in more than one problem. If that is the case, there will be a note stating "Questions —— through —— refer to the following figure."

A typical problem solving question is as follows:

At a rock concert, the ratio of girls to boys is 3:8. If there is a total of 54 girls, how many boys are there?

A. 144   D. 38
B. 133   E. Cannot be determined
C. 58

Finding the Answer

To answer a problem solving question, you should take the following approach:

Step One: *Read the entire question very carefully.* You may even wish to circle or underline some important information. If the problem is very long (such as a word problem), such notation can be quite helpful.

Step Two: *Determine exactly what the question is asking.* Do you have to find a percentage, a ratio, a total, or a fraction? Do you have to find a final solution or merely an intermediate step? Are you asked to find A's age or B's age? Be very careful to answer what the question is asking. Often the answer key will have specially written "trap" answers, answers that you might choose if you didn't read the question carefully.

Step Three: *Predict what you need to do to find the answer.* Note that this is different from actually doing the steps. Here, you want to determine how many calculations you have to make, how much time this problem is going to take, how hard it is going to be to solve. If you find that the problem is very hard, requiring skills you are weak in, you may want to postpone doing it until the end of the section. If you find that the problem is very simple, but will require several time-consuming steps, you will have to decide whether or not it is worth spending so much time on one problem.

Step Four: *Predict an answer form.* An answer form is not the answer itself; it is the form in which the answer will be given. For example, if you are asked to find the area of a figure, the form of the answer will be in square units. If you are asked to find the volume of a figure, the form of the answer will be in cubic units.

Step Five: *Look at the answer choices.* This step is critical. If you look at the answer choices, you can probably eliminate two or three answers immediately because they are in the wrong form (square units instead of cubic units, a fraction instead of a percentage). Looking at the answer choices will also allow you to determine how precisely you have to solve the problem. For example, if your answers are 0, 59, 199, 2,000, and 5,398,700, you know for certain that you can make a very rough estimate and still be correct. If the answers are 3, 4, 5, 6, 7 you know that you had better work the problem out precisely. *Do take the time to check over the answer choices before you begin your calculations.* You will be pleasantly surprised to find out how often you can do away with calculations entirely.

Step Six: *Solve the problem.* Occasionally, you will have to work out the entire problem. Remember, however, that the exam is not written to test your pencil-pushing abilities. The test makers do not want you to spend your time multiplying long numbers or adding many terms. They want to see whether you have the problem solving skills you will need for college. Therefore, if you find you are doing a great many calculations, you are probably missing short cuts or easily estimated solutions.

Using the Answer Choices

You have already learned the importance of looking at the answer choices *before* you begin doing your calculations. Doing so will allow you to eliminate answers that are in the wrong form. Doing so will also allow you to determine how precisely you will have to work the problem. Suppose, however, that looking at the answer choices only tells you that this problem has no short cuts, that you have to work it out entirely.

The answer choices can still help you in such a situation. You can use them to "work backwards" through the problem. For example, consider the ratio problem given at the beginning of this section. You should know (from having studied the review material from Day Three's lesson) that if the ratio of girls to boys is 3:8, there are 3 girls for every 8 boys. Since there are 54 girls, there are 18 groups or sets (54/3) of girls. Therefore, there must be 18 groups or sets of boys. Eighteen sets with 8 boys per set would give you the multiplication problem of 18 $\times$ 8. Although this is not an extremely hard problem, why do it? You know that the one's column is 8 $\times$ 8 and that 8 $\times$ 8 = 64. Therefore, the digit in the one's column must be a 4. Only the correct answer has that digit. This is an example of using the answer choices to prevent pencil-pushing, time-wasting activity on your part.

Traps to Avoid

With the problem solving *questions*, you should be careful to avoid the following traps:

1. *Do not make any assumptions as to what the question is asking.* Be very certain that you know whether you are being asked to find an intermediate step, a total, a percentage, a fraction, a volume, or an area. Determine whether you are being asked to find one value (such as A) or a double value (such as $2A$) or a partial value ($\frac{1}{2}A$). You may wish to circle or underline the exact item you are solving for. For example, in the ratio question given earlier, you may underline "how many boys" to remind yourself that you are not solving for a total number of boys and girls (another typical problem you will find on the exam), but just for the number of boys.

2. *Do not "mentally transfer" information from a preceding problem.* This happens frequently with geometry problems. Just because $X = 40$ in one problem does not mean it equals 40 in another geometry problem. Just because a variable was negative in one problem does not mean it is negative throughout the section. Unless a note tells you that a chart, graph, table, or figure is to be used in more than one problem, approach each problem as if it were the first.

3. *Do not choose "cannot be determined" or "not enough information" unless you are absolutely positive that the problem cannot be solved.* While these answers may be correct on certain problems, if you find that you are choosing them every time you see them, you are probably incorrect.

With the problem solving *answers*, you should be careful to avoid the following traps:

1. *Do not choose the first answer with the correct digits.* For example, answer A may say 64 feet, while answer D says 64 square feet. If you are solving for an area (which is always in square units), you would have to choose answer D. Check your units carefully. Take the few seconds necessary to skim all the answers.

2. *Be careful not to transpose numerals.* To transpose is to reverse the order of, such as writing 28 instead of 82. This error is made frequently by persons rushing to finish the last few problems. Often the answer choices deliberately have "variations on a theme," such as 276 and 267.

3. *Watch the decimal point placement.* An answer of 356.78 is vastly different from an answer of 35.678. Simply because the digits are correct does not mean you may choose an answer and go on to the next problem. Any time you have an answer with a decimal point, you should take extra care to slow down and look at the answer carefully.

Time-saving Suggestions

1. *Preview the problems.* Go directly to those you find relatively simple; save for last those with which you have dificulty. If you find symbolism problems hard but ratio problems simple, go directly to the ratio problems and leave the symbolism problems for the end. This way, if you do not finish the section, the problems you didn't do were the ones you would have done the worst on anyway. You may skip around within a section; just be careful not to lose your place on your answer grid.

2. *Estimate an answer whenever possible.* If you are able to determine that the answer must be within a certain range, you will probably be able to choose an answer from those given without having to do any exact calculations. Whenever possible, work backwards from the answer key rather than working through the whole problem.

3. *Reuse previous calculations.* Occasionally, there is no way to avoid working out specific operations. If you have to multiply 13 × 23 in one problem, chances are you will find that same calculation required later. Try to do your calculations neatly enough so that you can reread them later. Even if you do not have to use that exact same calculation, you may have to make one so close that you can use the previous one as a reference point for an estimation. For example, if you determined that 13 × 23 = 299; you can

estimate that 14 × 24 will be just a little larger. You do not have to multiply it out to find it is 336.

Practice Exam: Problem Solving

Please take the following practice exam on problem solving questions. As you learned earlier, problem solving questions are found in two separate sections of the SAT. One such section generally features 20 quantitative comparison questions along with 15 problem solving questions; the other section features 25 problem solving questions (and no QC questions). This practice exam follows the latter format. An answer key and explanatory answers follow this exam. Score yourself and remember: Incorrect answers cost you ¼ point each.

DIRECTIONS: Select the best answer to each problem. You may do any scratchwork directly on the exam. Circle the letter that appears before your choice.

1. Eight friends contribute the same amount of money to help pay the rent of a friend who is temporarily broke. When two more friends hear of this generosity, they insist on contributing too, making each person's gift total $80. By how much was each original contributor's donation decreased with the additional funds given by the two friends?

   A. $10   D. $35
   B. $20   E. $80
   C. $25

2. Richard paid $40 each for three shirts, then bought six more when they were reduced 37.5%. What was the average price paid per shirt?

   A. $46.90   D. $36.67
   B. $41.67   E. $30.00
   C. $39.54

3. What is the degree measure of arc *AC*?

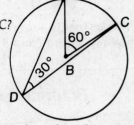

   A. 30°   D. 90°
   B. 40°   E. 100°
   C. 60°

4. How many prime numbers are in the set of numbers from 4 to 25?

   A. 26   D. 11
   B. 25   E. 7
   C. 13

5. The ratio of smokers to nonsmokers in a bar is 4:7. If there are 84 nonsmokers, how many people are there in the bar?

   A. 132   D. 84
   B. 123   E. Cannot be determined
   C. 110

6. What is the approximate measure of an angle in a regular heptagon?

   A. 150°   D. 94°
   B. 129°   E. 60°
   C. 102°

7. $\dfrac{X^{16}}{X^9} =$

   A. X^{25} D. X^2
   B. X^{96} E. X^{169}
   C. X^7

8. $W \# X \# Y \# Z = \dfrac{W}{X} + \dfrac{Y}{Z}$
   What is $2 \# 3 \# 4 \# 5$?

   A. 1⁷⁄₁₅   D. 2¹⁄₁₅
   B. 2⁷⁄₁₅   E. Cannot be determined
   C. 1²⁄₁₅

9. What is the rate of interest on a savings account that made $312 in a six-month period?

   A. 10% D. 15%
   B. 12% E. Cannot be determined
   C. 13%

10. Which of the following represents $(a - b)^2$?

    A. $a^2 + 2ab + b^2$ D. $a^2 + b^2$
    B. $a^2 - 2ab + b^2$ E. $a^2 - b^2$
    C. $a^2 + ab + b^2$

11. If an item cost $48.00 and sold for a 12.5% profit, what was the selling price of the item?

    A. $65.00 D. $50.13
    B. $54.00 E. $35.50
    C. $51.50

12. $38X - 14 = 19X + 100$. What is $33\frac{1}{3}\%X$?

    A. 114 B. 38 C. 19 D. 6 E. 2

13. Which of the following pieces of information is necessary to find the area of sector *AFB* in circle *F*?

    A. The degree measure of angle *EFB*
    B. The degree measure of angle *ADB*
    C. The radius of the circle
    D. All of the above
    E. None of the above

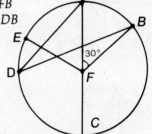

14. Which of the following represents the negative absolute value of negative three?

    A. $|-3|$ D. $-|-3|$
    B. $|3|$ E. None of the above
    C. $-|3|$

15. $10^4 - 10^{-1} =$

    A. 10,001   D. 9,999.9
    B. 10,100   E. 9,999.1
    C. 9,990

16. What is the perimeter of a 30°-60°-90° triangle with a height of 10?

    A. 180   D. $30 + 10 \sqrt{3}$
    B. 100   E. Cannot be determined
    C. $40 \sqrt{3}$

17. Every time Donovan made $10 on a bet, his friends Karl and Priscilla lost $25. If Donovan made $60, how much money did Priscilla lose?

    A. $150   D. $25
    B. $100   E. Cannot be determined
    C. $60

18. 38% of 41% of 68% of 100 = X. Which of the following is the closest approximation of X?

    A. .010   D. 10
    B. .1   E. 100
    C. 1.0

19. Achmed travels 60 mph for a third of an hour. His friend Moshe travels at 40% of that speed for six times as long. What fraction of the distance that Moshe travels is the distance that Achmed travels?

    A. $\frac{5}{12}$ D. ¾
    B. ½   E. $\frac{7}{9}$
    C. ⅖

20. Artificial turf for the high-school playing field costs $3.50 a square yard. If the field measures 150 × 60 feet but only a half of it will be covered with artificial turf, what will be the cost of the total amount of turf required?

A. $3,750   D. $1,750
B. $2,500   E. $1,250
C. $2,000

21. If $B = 2D$, $D = .40A$, $B = 133\frac{1}{3}\%C$, and $2E = D$, what is the value of C?

   A. ⅔   D. .4D
   B. ⅓B   E. 5A
   C. .6A

22. If $Z^4 = 1$, $Z =$

   A. 0   D. −1
   B. 4   E. 1 or −1
   C. 1

23. $\dfrac{\sqrt{6}\;\sqrt{24}}{\sqrt{4}} =$

   A. 12   D. 4
   B. 36   E. Cannot be determined
   C. 6

24. A compressor pushes air into a 250-liter container filling 40% of it in 20 seconds. What is the rate of flow of the air in liters per second?

   A. 5   D. 12
   B. 6   E. 25
   C. 10

25. At a rock concert, ⅔ of the fans are males and ⅔ of the males have shaved heads. Approximately what percent of the fans at the concert are males with shaved heads?

   A. 66⅔   D. 23
   B. 50   E. ⅘
   C. 44

ANSWER KEY

1. B	8. A	14. D	20. D
2. E	9. E	15. D	21. C
3. C	10. B	16. D	22. E
4. E	11. B	17. E	23. C
5. A	12. E	18. D	24. A
6. B	13. C	19. A	25. C
7. C			

Explanations

1. **(B)** When two friends join eight friends, there are 10 people; if each contributes $80, the total amount contributed is $800. If there were only the original eight friends, the total would still be $800, but each friend would have to pay ⅛, or $100. The difference between the amount paid per person with 10 people ($80) and the amount paid per person with eight people ($100) is $20.

2. **(E)** The first three shirts cost a total of $120. If a shirt is reduced by 37.5%, it is only 62.5% of its original price (because 100% − 37.5% = 62.5%). Since 62.5% = ⅝, you are trying to find what ⅝ of $40 is; it is $25. Six shirts at $25 each cost $150. $150 + $120 = $270. Divide the total, $270, by the number of shirts, 9, to get $30 per shirt.

3. **(C)** The degree measure of an arc is the same as the degree measure of the central angle opposite it. Here, the central angle (the one having the midpoint of the circle as its vertex) is 60°; therefore, the arc is 60° as well.

4. **(E)** Prime numbers are any numbers that may be divided evenly only by themselves and 1. The prime numbers between 4 and 25 are (5, 7, 11, 13, 17, 19, 23).

5. **(A)** Think of the ratio as telling you how many persons are in a set; there are 4 persons in a set of smokers and 7 persons in a set of nonsmokers. Since there are 84 nonsmokers, there are 12 *sets* (84/7) of nonsmokers. There must then be 12 sets of smokers. With 4 people to a set, there are 48 (4 × 12) smokers. 84 + 48 = 132.

6. **(B)** Find the total degree measure of all of the interior angles with the formula $(S - 2)$ $(180°)$, with S representing the number of sides of the figure. A heptagon has 7 sides; therefore you multiply $(7 - 2)$ or 5 by 180° to get 900°. Since a *regular* polygon has all equal sides and all equal angles, divide the total by the number of angles. $900/7 = 128.57$ or approximately 129°.

7. **(C)** When dividing like bases with different exponents (the X is the base; the number is the exponent), subtract the exponents. $16 - 9 = 7$.

8. **(A)** The # is a symbol. The first part of the problem tells you how to use the symbol; you make a fraction of the first two numbers, then add it to a fraction made of the second two numbers. You may also think of this problem as substituting the 2 for the W, the 3 for the X, the 4 for the Y, and the 5 for the Z. This gives you $\frac{2}{3} + \frac{4}{5}$. Use the common denominator of 15 to get $\frac{10}{15} + \frac{12}{15} = \frac{22}{15}$ or $1\frac{7}{15}$.

9. **(E)** The formula needed here is $I = PRT$ (Interest equals Principal times Rate times Time). Here, you are given the interest earned and the time but are not given either the principal or the rate. To get the rate, you would need to be given the principal. Since the principal is not given here, the answer cannot be determined.

10. **(B)** Work through the problem as shown below, taking one variable at a time and multiplying it by the others. Note that $-ab$ and $-ba$ are the same; any two numbers may be multiplied in any order (such as 6×5 or 5×6).

$$
\begin{aligned}
(a - b)(a - b) \\
a \cdot a = a^2 \\
a \cdot -b = -ab \\
-b \cdot a = -ba \\
\underline{-b \cdot -b = +b^2} \\
a^2 - 2ab + b^2
\end{aligned}
$$

11. **(B)** The formula needed here is $S = C + P$, Sales price equals Cost plus Profit. The profit is 12.5%, which is the same as $\frac{1}{8}$. One-eighth of the cost is $6. Add the profit of $6 to the cost of

$48 to get the selling price of $54. Note that you could automatically have eliminated answer E. The selling price must be *more* than the cost, since the question tells you that a profit (rather than a loss) occurred.

12. **(E)** This is a simple algebra question that you could easily have missed had you been careless and not read what the question wanted you to solve for. You are not giving an answer of "X = . . ." but an answer of "33⅓% X = . . ." First, find for X. Move all the X terms to one side and all the non-X terms to the other. Move the 19X to the left, making it −19X (remember that when you move a term from one side of the equal sign to the other, you change its sign—a positive becomes a negative and a negative becomes a positive). Move the −14 to the right of the equal sign, making it +14. Combine like terms: 38X − 19X = 19X. 100 + 14 = 114. (Note that 114 is one of the trap answers.) Divide both sides through by 19 in order to get an X by itself. $^{19X}/_{19}$ = X; $^{114}/_{19}$ = 6. You now know that X = 6; However, remember that the question wants to know what 33⅓% X is. Since 33⅓% is the same as ⅓, you can determine that ⅓ X is the same as $^{X}/_{3}$, or $^{6}/_{3}$ = 2. You didn't fall into the trap and put answer D, did you?

13. **(C)** In order to find the area of a sector, you need to have two pieces of information: the fraction that the sector is of the area of the circle (found by knowing the fraction that the central angle is of the total degree measure of the circle) and the area of the circle. In this case you have the former and only need the latter. Answer A is incorrect because the sector *AFB* has nothing to do with angle *EFB*. If you wanted to find the area of sector *EFB*, rather than of sector *AFB*, you would need that angle. Here, it is irrelevant. Answer B is a little more useful, but not *necessary*. Since angle *ADB* has the same intercepted arc (arc *AB*) as angle *AFB*, you know that angle *ADB* has ½ the degree measure of angle *AFB*. If you didn't know the degree measure of angle *AFB*, knowing the degree measure of angle *ADB* would be critical. However, since the problem tells you the measure of *AFB* is 30°, you don't need to know the measure of angle *ADB*. Answer C is correct. Since you still must find the area of the circle, you have to have some

linear measurement that would allow you to find it. You could have the radius or the diameter or the longest chord. With the radius you could find the area and multiply it by the fraction that angle *AFB* is of the circle.

14. **(D)** The absolute value is the magnitude of a number, the number of actual units regardless of the positive or negative status. Absolute value is represented by two vertical lines, such that |5| would be read as "the absolute value of 5." Absolute values are always given as positive. |−5| would be read as "the absolute value of negative 5," but the answer would be 5, not negative 5. Answer A represents the absolute value of negative 3. Answer B represents the absolute value of positive 3. Answer C represents the negative absolute value of positive 3. Answer D is correct; it represents the negative absolute value of negative 3.

15. **(D)** Ten to the fourth is 10,000. Ten to the negative first is the same as ¹⁄₁₀, or .1. 10,000 − .1 = 9,999.9. Note how the other answers are all devious; if you chose any of them, you probably tried to do this problem too quickly. Remember that you should look at the answer key *before* doing the problem. Had you done so in this instance, you would have noted that the answers are all pretty close and rather tricky. Because of this, you should have slowed down, taken the time to write out the problem and actually do the math visually, rather than just in your head.

16. **(D)** Since one of the angles is 90°, the triangle is a right triangle, allowing you to find the measures of the sides using the Pythagorean Theorem. With a 30°-60°-90° triangle, there is a special 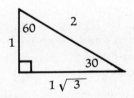 ratio for the lengths of the sides. It is $1:1\sqrt{3}:2$. Since the height is the same as the side opposite the 30° angle, it is represented by the "1" in the ratio (see figure). That means that the sides are $10:10\sqrt{3}:20$. Add the 10 and the 20 to get 30.

You cannot add the $10\sqrt{3}$ to get $40\sqrt{3}$; you may only add it as is, "$10\sqrt{3}$" Your final answer is $30 + 10\sqrt{3}$.

17. **(E)** The question gives you a ratio of the winning of Donovan to the losing of Karl and Priscilla. You could find out how much Karl *and* Priscilla lost when Donovan won $60; however, you cannot isolate Priscilla and find out how much she alone lost. You have no idea of the financial situation between Karl and Priscilla (perhaps they lost an equal amount, perhaps one lost more than the other, you just don't know). You do not have enough information and cannot solve the problem.

18. **(D)** Work backwards. Sixty-eight percent of 100 is 68. Quickly take 40% (since the question only asks for an approximation you should simplify your multiplication) of 68 to get about 27. Then take about 40% again to get about 10. Note that the answers in your answer key are all based on the digits 1 and 0; you merely had to find the "placeholders" to determine whether your answer would be 10, 1, or less than 1. You should have eliminated answer E immediately; obviously a (less than 100) percentage of 100 must be less than 100.

	TIME	RATE	DISTANCE
A	⅓ hr	60 mph	20 mi
M	2 hr	24 mph	48 mi

19. **(A)** Draw yourself a time/rate/distance chart as indicated. Remember that the formula is that Rate times Time equals Distance. If Achmed travels at 60 mph for a third of an hour, he goes 20 miles. Moshe travels at 40% of that speed, or 24 mph for six times as long, or for 2 hours (6 times ⅓ hour= 2 hours). Moshe therefore travels (2 × 24=) 48 miles. The distance that Achmed travels (20 miles) is ⁵⁄₁₂ of the distance that Moshe travels (48 miles). (²⁰⁄₄₈ = ¹⁰⁄₂₄ = ⁵⁄₁₂)

20. **(D)** The key to this question is noting that the measurements of the field are given in feet while the cost of the turf is given in yards. Convert feet to yards by dividing by 3 (since there are 3 feet in a yard). That means the field is 50 yards by 20 yards. Multiply these figures together to get an area of 1,000

square yards. Since only half the field will be covered, you only need to multiply 500 by the cost per square yard ($3.50) to get a total of $1,750.

21. **(C)** Make a small chart or "order line" for yourself, using the information given. Frequently, beginning at the *end* of the problem is best. Here, you have $2E = D$. Assign hypothetical values to make working with these numbers easier. Say that $E = 1$.

A = 5
B = 4
C = 3
D = 2
E = 1

Then $D = 2$. Skip now to the next piece of information with a D: $D = .40A$. Since .40 is the same as $\frac{2}{5}$, $D = \frac{2}{5}A$; $A = 5$. You are told that $B = 2D$; therefore, $B = 4$. Finally, you are given information that B (which is 4) $= 133 \frac{1}{3}\%$ (or $1\frac{1}{3}$ times) C. This makes $C = 3$. You now have all your information: $A = 5$; $B = 4$; $C = 3$; $D = 2$; $E = 1$. Your last step is to look at the answer choices and see which correctly represents the value of C. Since C is 3 and A is 5, $C = .6$ (which is the same as $\frac{3}{5}$) A.

22. **(E)** Z to the fourth power means $Z \times Z \times Z \times Z$. The only way to get a 1 when the same number is multiplied by itself is to begin with a 1 or a -1. Since any negative number to an even power is positive, Z could be $+1$ *or* -1. Note that if the question said that Z cubed were 1, Z could only be $+1$, not -1.

23. **(C)** When multiplying or dividing with radicals (the numbers here with the square root signs), ignore the sign. Perform the operations, then replace the sign. Here, multiply 6×24 to get 144. Now, you have two choices. You can replace the radical sign, such that you have $\sqrt{144} / \sqrt{4}$, and find the square roots to get 12 (since 12 is the square root of 144) divided by 2 (since 2 is the square root of 4). Reduce that to 6. Or, you could ignore the radical signs, divide 144 by 4 to get 36, then replace the radical sign. The square root of $36 = 6$. Either way will give you the correct answer.

24. **(A)** Forty percent of the container is filled in 20 seconds; 40% of 250 $= 100$. If 100 liters are filled in 20 seconds, then ($\frac{100}{20}=$) 5 liters are filled in one second. The rate is 5 liters per second.

25. **(C)** To find a fraction of a fraction ($\frac{2}{3}$ of the $\frac{2}{3}$), multiply the numbers together (remember that *of* signifies multiplication).

Multiply the numerators to get (2 × 2 =) 4; multiply the denominators to get (3 × 3 =)9. $\frac{4}{9}$ is $.\overline{4444}$ or approximately 44%.

NUMBER RIGHT:____(Give yourself one point for each.)

NUMBER WRONG:____(Multiply by ¼ point each.)

FINAL SCORE:____(Subtract the second number from the first; you may have an answer with a fraction, such as 17½.)

5.

Day Five

Hour One: Usage

Set Your Clock. *This first hour of today's lesson covers the first of two types of questions you will find on the Test of Standard Written English (TSWE): the usage question. The second hour of today's lesson covers the other question type found on the TSWE: the Sentence Correction question.*

What You Will See

The entire TSWE consists of 50 questions. Generally, questions 1–25 are usage, questions 26–40 are sentence correction, and questions 41–50 are usage. Please note that the usage questions appear both before and after the sentence correction questions. Some students have made the mistake of thinking they were finished when they did the last sentence correction question; be certain to turn the page and look for the final 10 usage questions.

The Question Format. Each usage question is a sentence with five underlined portions. Four of the underlined portions are parts of the sentence. Each "part" may be a punctuation mark (such as a semicolon), a word or words, a phrase or a clause. The fifth portion follows the sentence; the words "No error" are written at the end of every sentence.

Below each underlined portion is a letter, A–E. You are to choose the underlined portion that must be changed in order to make the sentence correct. Write the letter below that portion on your answer grid. Note that if no portion of the sentence needs to be changed, you choose answer E, "No error."

An example of a usage question is as follows:

I <u>really</u> don't know <u>who</u> to blame<u> ;</u> I think <u>we are</u> all guilty of
   A   B   C   D

neglect. <u>No error</u>
         E

Read the entire sentence before choosing your answer. Note the underlined portions. A is correct; "really" is the proper adverb modifying the verb "don't know." B is wrong (and therefore is the answer you select). "Who" should be "whom" as the word is the object of the verb "to blame." Since "who" is subjective and must serve as the subject of a sentence or clause, it is incorrect. Answer C is correct; a semicolon (;) does connect two independent sentences. (You may test to see whether sentences are independent by writing each one alone. Since "I really don't know whom to blame" and "I think we are all guilty of neglect" each is able to stand alone as a complete sentence, each is independent.) Answer D is correct; "we are" has the proper subject (the pronoun "we" is in the subjective case; had the pronoun been "us," which is in the objective case, it would have been incorrect) and the proper verb (since "we" is plural, the verb "are" which is plural is correct). Since there is an error in the sentence, do not choose answer E, "No error." B is the proper answer.

NOTE: You should always read the *entire* sentence. This is so because while the majority of the errors will be grammatical, some will be errors in logic or meaning. Unless you understand the overall meaning of the sentence, you might miss such errors. Read the whole sentence first, then look again at the underlined portions.

Ordering the Questions

Many students find it is best to do all of the usage questions first, then go back and do the sentence correction questions. Following this procedure has two benefits: first, you guarantee that you do not neglect to do the final 10 usage questions; second, you may keep your mind on one question style at a time, rather than jumping from one type to another. However, if you do all of the usage questions first, *be very careful to mark the correct spaces on your answer grid.* Remember that you will be skipping questions; do not mark your grid from 1–35, but from 1–25 and from 41–50.

The Best Approach

1. *As you have already learned, read the entire sentence first.* Doing so will allow you to grasp the overall meaning, logic, and structure of the sentence. Some errors can be very tricky; understanding the organization of the sentence allows you to recognize them more easily.

2. *Look for obvious grammatical errors.* Usually, the majority of the errors in this portion of the TSWE are basic grammatical ones. For example, usage questions often test commonly confused pairs of words such as "lie/lay," "rise/raise/," "sit/set," and "affect/effect." Whenever you see one of these "key" words, double check it.

3. *Look for structural errors.* A structural error is a problem in the format of the sentence. For example, the sentence might be a fragment (an incomplete sentence, a portion rather than a whole sentence) or a run-on (two or more sentences incorrectly joined). When there is a structural error, often the error is easy to recognize but hard to translate into a correct answer (that is, you know the sentence is a fragment, but you don't know which underlined portion is incorrect). For example, the sentence, "While Diana was walking down the street last weekend, stopping every now and then to smell the roses" is a fragment; it does not express a complete thought. To make the sentence correct (complete), you would eliminate the word "while." ("Diana was walking along the street last weekend, stopping every now and then to smell the roses" is a complete sentence; it finishes a thought.)

4. *Look for logical inconsistencies.* A logical inconsistency is often a mistake in gender, number, or tense. For example, if the sentence begins by referring to the teacher as a "he" then halfway through begins referring to that same teacher as a "she," you have an inconsistency. If the beginning of the sentence refers to just one person while the second part of the sentence uses the pronoun "they" (which is plural and refers to more than one person), you

have an inconsistency. If the sentence refers to something that happened during the time of King Arthur but uses the verb "is," (rather than the past tense, "was"), you have an inconsistency. Often these errors are especially hard to find because the words are not themselves incorrect (there is nothing wrong with the word "is," per se; it was simply used incorrectly in the example above). Reading the entire sentence to get the overall idea of it helps you locate these errors.

Trouble Areas

Suppose that you have read and reread a sentence and just know that something is wrong, but you can't quite put your finger on what it is. What do you do now? You do not choose "No error," answer E, giving up without a fight. Try the following to diagnose the error.

1. *Go through a grammatical checklist in your mind.* When you have finished the practice exam after this section (and the one after the sentence correction section as well), you will have learned a number of grammatical rules. Write them down on index cards, learn them, and organize them into a checklist that you can go through rapidly on the actual exam. For example, part of your checklist might read like this:

   a. subject/verb agreement
   b. pronoun number/clarity/gender
   c. commonly misused words (e.g., "lie/lay")
   d. sentence structure

Of course, your checklist would be longer; this is just an example. Having such a checklist is a wonderful idea. It gives you something concrete to use, something specific to help you get a handle on the question. Most of the time an error will "jump out at you," will be very obvious. Your checklist will help you find the errors that are not so obvious.

2. *Rewrite the sentence in your mind.* If you think the sentence is awkward but you don't know which underlined portion is incor-

rect, rewrite the sentence to yourself. Don't change the meaning of the sentence, just its style and organization. When you have rewritten the sentence, compare it to the original. Most likely you will find that the difference between the two is the error you are seeking.

Traps to Avoid

1. *Do not misread the sentence.* This is one of the most common errors made by students who are rushed during an exam. Do not read the sentence as you think it "should be"; read it as it is. If the sentence says, "Matilda don't like wearing shoes," *don't* automatically read, "Matilda doesn't like wearing shoes." Go slowly enough to be certain you are not substituting your own words for those written on the exam.

2. *Do not assume that "trap" or "trick" expressions are necessarily wrong.* For example, the words "who" and "whom" are frequently tested. Don't see one of those words and think you have found the error; who or whom could be used incorrectly *or* correctly. You have a 50-50 chance.

3. *Do not assume that words whose meanings you do not know are incorrectly used.* For example, if the sentence uses the word "dichotomy" and you don't know its meaning, don't say that the word must be wrong. Even if you are certain that the rest of the sentence is correct, don't think that by process of elimination, the "big" word must be wrong. Remember that you could always have a sentence with no error.

Time-saving Suggestions

1. *Do all the usage questions first, then go back and do the sentence correction questions.* Since each usage question is only one sentence long, while each sentence correction question is one sentence with five additional sentences or portions of sentences (as you will see when you do the next hour's lesson), you probably will be able to

do the usage questions much more rapidly than the sentence correction questions. If you should happen to run out of time at the end of the section, you may only have four or five sentence correction questions left undone. Had you run out of time after doing all the sentence correction questions, you may find that you have all 10 of the remaining usage questions (remember that 10 additional usage questions follow the sentence correction questions) left undone.

2. *Read the sentence slowly the first time.* This may sound like an unusual tip to put into a "time-saving" section, but reading a sentence right the first time will save you precious time later. Generally, if you misread a sentence, you will fret and worry over what could be wrong (most people who misread a sentence do so by correcting any errors that are there, turning the sentence into a "No error" question) and will spend twice as much time on it as you should. Verbalize the question (that is, slowly read it with your lips forming the words; do not merely skim the question with your eyes) to help yourself find errors on the first try.

3. *Skip any questions you find wholly confusing.* If you read a sentence and know that something is wrong and you have tried the suggestions given above (such as rewriting the sentence in your mind) to no avail, skip the question and go on to the next one. There are so many questions in this section that you do not have time to agonize over just one. Be very careful, however, to skip a space on your answer grid as well so that you won't end up misnumbering answers all the way through the rest of the section.

Practice Exam: Usage

Please take the following practice exam on usage questions. This practice exam consists of 35 questions with an answer key and explanatory answers following. Score yourself and remember: Incorrect answers cost you ¼ point each!

DIRECTIONS: The following sentences test your understanding of
and ability to use standard written English. While a sentence may
have no errors, no sentence has more than one error. The errors
are in grammar, usage, diction (word choice), and idiomatic construction.

Any error will be underlined and lettered. Any nonunderlined
portions of the sentence must be assumed to be correct. If there is
an error, choose as your answer the underlined portion that must
be changed to make the sentence correct. Circle the letter below
your answer.

1.   Some of the friends at the slumber party that Sharon
       gave last weekend was unable to get more than a few
        A   B   C
       hours sleep due to all the talking. No error
                          D   E

2.   Just between you and I, I think that the best teacher
                       A   B
       in the school is Jay Ward, who makes even poetry fas-
                      C   D
       cinating. No error
                 E

3.   Selling surplus goods at swap meets, a good way to
       A   B
       clean out your attic and garage and make a little extra
                                                 C
       money at the same time. No error
              D   E

4.   During the past decade, my parents found that the
       A
       majority of teachers of mine that they liked are those
                                                    B
       who took the time to explain exactly what they were
       B   C   D
       teaching and why. No error
                        E

5. $\underline{\text{I know}}$ Mrs. Foxworthy tries $\underline{\text{her best}}$ to $\underline{\text{arrive}}$
      A   B   C

promptly, but it seems as if she $\underline{\text{is late everytime}}$ she
   C   D

drives. $\underline{\text{No error}}$
          E

6.   Clarence N. Blake and Donald F. Martin $\underline{\text{who wrote}}$
                                                  A

a very $\underline{\text{interesting}}$ book $\underline{\text{on the accomplishments}}$ of
           B   C

$\underline{\text{famous}}$ blacks. $\underline{\text{No error}}$
   D   E

7.   Either the new cat or the old dog $\underline{\text{have}}$ $\underline{\text{to be}}$ $\underline{\text{given}}$
                                            A   B   C

$\underline{\text{away;}}$ the pets simply do not get along together.
   D

$\underline{\text{No error}}$
   E

8.   The bacteria $\underline{\text{was}}$ found $\underline{\text{to be}}$ growing and repro-
      A   B

ducing at a frightening rate, $\underline{\text{prompting some}}$ scientists
                                        C

to $\underline{\text{cancel}}$ the experiment. $\underline{\text{No error}}$
      D   E

9. $\underline{\text{Each of us}}$ in the girl scout troup $\underline{\text{was told}}$ to be cer-
      A   B

tain $\underline{\text{to have our permission}}$ slip signed by at least one
         C

parent and returned to the teacher $\underline{\text{no later than}}$ Friday.
                                            D

$\underline{\text{No error}}$
   E

10. No one knows whom the next student council presi-
        A   B

dent will be; all the candidates this year are both popu-
                              C   D

lar and qualified. No error
                 E

11. Jane Matilda Bolin was the first black female judge
                       A   B   C

in America she was appointed to the court of domestic
                   D

relations by Mayor La Guardia of New York in 1939.

No error
  E

12. When we saw poor Jacob laying on the ground
                            A

holding his leg and groaning, we all feared that he
  B   C

had sustained a serious injury. No error
   D   E

13. My mother says that Bessie Smith was as talented, if
  A   B   C   D

not more talented than, Billie Holiday. No error
                                  E

14. The bluebird and it's mate spent hours building a
               A   B   C

nest in the tree outside my bedroom window. No error
                       D   E

15. One must be certain to study sufficiently to do well
                     A   B

on a test, otherwise you might flunk and have to go
                         C

through all that trouble again. No error
                       D   E

16.   Wang Chung <u>was speaking</u> so <u>loud</u> that <u>we could</u>
                          A   B   C
hear his voice over the public address system, <u>the</u>
 C   D
<u>band,</u> and the wailing of a nearby baby! <u>No error</u>
 D   E

17.   Interest rates <u>have risen</u> so <u>quickly</u> that my father
                            A   B
is not certain he can afford to take out a loan <u>to send</u>
                                                        C
me to an Ivy League college this <u>year; I may</u> have
                                          D
to go to State. <u>No error</u>
                    E

18.   <u>The main</u> idea of the seminars <u>offered by</u> the several
         A   B
departments of the various colleges <u>are</u> that students
                                          C
should have the right <u>to vote</u> whether a teacher be
                            D
given tenure or not. <u>No error</u>
                          E

19.   <u>Forced</u> <u>to choose</u> <u>among</u> an opera and a country and
         A   B   C
western songfest, Regina chose the <u>latter</u>. <u>No error</u>
                                         D   E

20.   Joe Namath <u>was</u> a football player <u>who was</u> famous
                      A   B
for his <u>masculine virility</u> and his <u>excellent</u> passing arm.
             C   D
<u>No error</u>
 E

21.   When our pep squad <u>screamed and begged</u> the
                                         A
       football team <u>to make</u> a touchdown, the team seemed
                         B
       to get <u>its</u> second wind and went and <u>did it</u>.
                 C   D
       <u>No error</u>
          E

22.   The admission committee of the community college
       <u>rarely</u> <u>have</u> a full <u>agenda</u> as everyone is automatically
          A   B   C
       admitted to the school <u>upon application</u>. <u>No error</u>
                                      D   E

23.   The disco dance halls <u>seem</u> <u>to see</u> <u>less and less</u> stu-
                                  A   B   C
       dents right <u>around the time</u> of final exams. <u>No error</u>
                          D   E

24.   <u>Cheryl said that</u> she <u>had heard hardly nothing</u> from
              A   B
       her brother <u>since</u> he joined the Navy <u>and</u> was shipped
                       C   D
       out to Hong Kong. <u>No error</u>
                              E

25.   <u>Winning the first place</u> medal <u>was</u> a relief to Samuel
                 A   B
       as he <u>had began</u> questioning whether he would ever
       C   D
       beat Nigel in a race again. <u>No error</u>
                                       E

26.   At <u>every</u> football game, <u>there are</u> <u>a few of we</u> sup-
           A   B   C
       porters <u>who</u> will cheer every play, even if the team is
                  D
       losing the game. <u>No error</u>
                            E

27.   Although she had done good on her earlier exam,
           A   B   C
Dotty flunked the next two due to a lack of concentra-
                              D
tion. No error
      E

28.   When I saw the teacher shake his head and wag his
                                A
finger at me, I implied that he had seen me sneak a
              B   C
peek at the paper of the boy next to me. No error
D   E

29.   Disaster seemed immanent; fortunately, at the last
                         A   B
minute my father helped me out and baked a cake
B
of his own that I could submit for my final project.
                  C   D
No error
E

30.   I couldn't believe my ears when I got a complement
      A   B   C
from the cutest boy in class because I thought he didn't
           D
know I was alive! No error
                  E

31.   Ms. Christie and him were the star speakers at the
           A   B   C
mystery writers' convention, held in Whodunit, Ten-
                 D
nessee. No error
        E

32.   Many teachers get a feeling of satisfaction when
                      A

they're students come back to them years later just to
     B   C   D

say hello. No error
           E

33.   Over a thousand years ago, the only way of preserv-
                  A

ing foods is by rolling them in spices or smoking them.
         B   C   D

No error
  E

34.   The student body government insists that they get
                                A   B

recognition in the school newspaper. No error
    C   D   E

35.   Running Wolf's speech was on the history of Native
                        A

Americans which had been persecuted for years.
          B   C   D

No error
  E

USAGE ANSWER KEY

1. B	10. B	19. C	28. B
2. A	11. D	20. C	29. A
3. B	12. A	21. D	30. C
4. B	13. D	22. B	31. A
5. D	14. A	23. C	32. B
6. A	15. C	24. B	33. B
7. A	16. B	25. D	34. B
8. A	17. E	26. C	35. B
9. C	18. C	27. C	

Explanations

1. **(B)** The subject of the sentence is *some*, which is one of the "special subjects." The special subjects are words that take

their number from the words following them. The special subjects are *some, any, most, all, none.* With these words, you look at the noun following each one. If that noun is plural, you need a plural verb. If that noun is singular, you need a singular verb. Here, some is followed by friends ("some of the friends"); since friends is plural, you must have a plural verb, "were," not "was."

2. **(A)** "Between" is a preposition; a noun or pronoun that follows it is the object of the preposition and must be in the objective case. Here, "I" is one of the objects of the preposition ("you" is the other object) but is in the subjective case. Change "I" to "me" to make the pronoun objective and correct.

3. **(B)** The "sentence" as written is actually a fragment, an incomplete sentence. It does not express a complete thought. Change portion B to read, "*is* a good way" to make the sentence correct. *Be careful:* On a sentence of this sort, do not read so quickly that you accidentally supply words that are not printed, making you think that the sentence is correct. Read only what is printed.

4. **(B)** Since the entire sentence is in a frame of reference of the past ("during the past decade"), the verb must be in the past as well. My parents found that the teachers they liked *were* those who took the time, etc.

5. **(D)** There is no such word as "everytime." The correct expression is two words, "every time."

6. **(A)** The "sentence" as written is incomplete; it is a fragment, not expressing a complete thought. Remove the word "who" to make the sentence "whole" and correct.

7. **(A)** With either/or or neither/nor, whatever noun or pronoun follows the "or" or the "nor" determines the number of the verb. In other words, if you have a singular word following the "or," you must use a singular verb. If you have a plu-

ral word following the "or," you must use a plural verb. This is true regardless of whether the word following the "either" is singular or plural. Since the word following the "or" in this instance is singular ("*or* the old dog"; dog is singular), you need a singular verb, "has."

8. **(A)** "Bacteria" is plural. You need the plural verb, "were." Other nouns that have unusual singular/plural forms are "media" (plural)/"medium" (singular) and "phenomena" (plural)/"phenomenon" (singular).

9. **(C)** The subject is each, which is singular. "Each of us *was* told" (the verb is singular and is correct). However, the pronoun, "our," is plural and is incorrect. Since the subject and verb are singular, the pronoun must be singular as well. Portion C should read, "to have her permission" (use the feminine pronoun since you are talking about members of a girl scout troup).

10. **(B)** "Whom" is incorrect here; "who" must be used. The "who" is actually a predicate nominative (a noun in the predicate) following the connecting or linking verb, "be." When you have two portions of a sentence connected by any form of the verb to be (such as is, are, was, were, etc.) you must connect two words in the subjective case. Since whom is objective, it is incorrect here.

11. **(D)** The sentence is a run-on; it has two independent sentences incorrectly joined. You could make the run-on into two sentences: ". . . the first black female judge in America. She was appointed . . ." or you could use a semicolon (;) to connect the two independent sentences ". . . the first black female judge in America; she was appointed . . ."

12. **(A)** Portion A should be "lying" not "laying." To lie is to recline, to rest. To lay is to put or place and requires an object (you must lay something down, such as laying the keys on the table).

13. **(D)** The correct expression is, "as talented *as*, if not more talented than." The second *as* is missing, making the comparison incomplete. Remember to read the sentence slowly and carefully in order to catch "missing" words; do not subconsciously supply the word yourself.

14. **(A)** Portion A is incorrect here. "It's" with an apostrophe is a contraction of "it is." You may say, "It's lucky I studied hard for this exam." "Its" with no apostrophe is the possessive form of it. You may say, "The book was losing its pages from overuse."

15. **(C)** Use either "one" or "you" throughout a sentence; you cannot change from one form to another halfway through. Since the nonunderlined portions of the sentence (which you are told must be correct) use one, use one throughout.

16. **(B)** The word "loud" is an adjective and modifies a noun. Here, it is incorrect because it is modifying a verb, speaking (it tells *how* the man was speaking). Therefore, the adverb loudly is needed.

17. **(E)** The sentence is correct. Two concepts were being tested: rise/raise and the semicolon. Rise is correctly used because it requires no object (something rises of its own accord, such as the sun rising or interest rates rising). The word "raise" would be correct only if followed by an object: one raises *something* (raise your grade). The semicolon is correct as it connects two independent sentences.

18. **(C)** The subject is the main idea, and is singular. It requires a singular verb, is, not the plural verb, are. All the prepositional phrases with their plural objects ("seminars," "departments," "colleges") do *not* affect subject/verb agreement.

19. **(C)** Among is used to compare more than two; between is used to compare exactly two. Since exactly two items are being compared here (an opera and a country and western songfest), *between* is required. Note that another concept was

being tested: *latter*. Latter is the comparative form and compares exactly two items. Therefore it is correctly used here. The superlative form, last, would be used to compare more than two items.

20. **(C)** Virility is the quality of masculinity, so the expression "masculine virility" is redundant. You could say that Mr. Namath was known for his masculinity or for his virility; do not use both terms together.

21. **(D)** Portion D should read, "and did *so.*" *So* is used to refer to actions, such as making a touchdown. *It* is used to refer to specific things or items ("I want the book; where is it?")

22. **(B)** The subject is the "committee." Committee is a collective noun. It looks plural but is actually singular (some of the other collective nouns frequently tested are government, union, club, and organization). Therefore, a singular verb is needed, "has," not "have."

23. **(C)** "Less" is an adjective used before a singular noun, such as less time or less work. "Fewer" is an adjective used before a plural noun, such as "fewer" hours or "fewer" jobs. Since you are referring to the plural "students" here, you need "fewer."

24. **(B)** "Hardly nothing" is a double negative (you may not use two negatives together; they change the meaning from negative to positive). The proper expression is "hardly anything."

25. **(D)** There is no such expression as "had began." You either use the simple past, "began," ("Jane began her job yesterday") or use the auxiliary verb "had" with "begun" ("Jane already had begun her job by the time I moved to the city"). In this sentence, "had begun" would be correct.

26. **(C)** In portion C, "we" is the object of the preposition "of" and should be in the objective case, "us." In a phrase of this sort, the easiest thing to do is to eliminate the noun following

the pronoun and read the sentence aloud. You would not say, "... there are a few of we" but you would say, "... there are a few of us."

27. **(C)** "Good" is an adjective and modifies a noun or pronoun. The adverb "well" is needed here because it modifies the action of the verb, "had done," telling "how" Dotty had done.

28. **(B)** To imply is to suggest. To infer is to deduce, to conclude. One infers in one's own mind. Here, the speaker infers that he has been caught because he deduces or concludes that in his own mind.

29. **(A)** "Immanent" means inherent, inborn. The word needed here is "imminent," meaning impending, likely to happen soon.

30. **(C)** To complement is to complete; a complement is a completing portion (such as a 40-degree angle being the complement to a 50-degree angle). The word needed here is "compliment." To compliment is to praise; a compliment is a word of praise.

31. **(A)** The subject is Ms. Christie and *him*, but "him" is in the objective, not subjective, case. You need Ms. Christie and *he*. In a situation of this sort, it is often advisable to ignore the other subject and just read the sentence with the tested word. You would not say, "him was the star speaker," but you would say, "he was the star speaker."

32. **(B)** "They're" is a contraction of "they are." "Their" is the possessive form of "they" and is needed here.

33. **(B)** The tense of the verb in portion B is incorrect. "Is" is the present tense, but the sentence is talking about something that happened in the past, over a thousand years ago. The past tense, was, is required.

34. **(B)** Government is a collective noun; it looks plural but is actually singular. You must follow it with a singular verb (insists

is correct in this sentence) and a singular pronoun (they is in-correct; use it).

35. **(B)** Native Americans are *people;* people must be referred to with a "who," "whom," or (occasionally) "that." They may not be referred to with a *which.*

NUMBER RIGHT:____(Give yourself one point for each.)

NUMBER WRONG:____(Multiply by ¼ point each.)

FINAL SCORE:____(Subtract the second number from the first; you may have an answer with a fraction, such as 27½.)

Hour Two: Sentence Correction

Set Your Clock. In the first hour of today's lesson, you learned about usage questions, the first type of grammar question found in the TSWE portion of the SAT. This hour's lesson covers the second type of grammar question found in that same section, the sentence correction question.

What You Will See

As you learned before, the TSWE has 50 questions. Generally, 15 of those will be sentence correction, with the remaining 35 usage.

The Question Format. Each sentence correction question consists of a sentence; either part or all of that sentence will be underlined. Following the sentence are five ways to state the underlined portion. NOTE: The first way, A, is identical to the original. You only choose that answer if you wish to state that the original is the best way of writing the sentence.

You should read the entire sentence in each instance. Do not read only the underlined portion; usually, it will make sense only in the context of the sentence itself. Do *not* skim the entire sentence and read only the underlined portion carefully. Since you are to choose a portion which is both grammatically correct and *logical* within the context of the sentence, you must understand the entire sentence. Thinking that you can save time by concentrating only on the underlined portion is a major mistake.

An example of a sentence correction question is as follows:

My sister, <u>who I have never understood at all,</u> wants to join my company; however, I don't think I will allow her to do so.

A. who I have never understood at all
B. who I never have understood at all
C. who I never understand at all
D. whom I have never understood at all
E. whom I never understand

Note how much of the sentence is underlined. While you should read the entire sentence, you may change only the underlined portion. It is very important that you understand this. Even if you feel that there are errors in the nonunderlined portions (there will *not* be specific errors, but you may think that those portions could be better written) you may not change them. You must *understand* the whole sentence; you may *change* only the underlined portion.

CAUTION: Be certain to note *exactly* how much of the sentence is underlined. Although this is not a problem in the above example, there may be instances in which the underlining or nonunderlining of a period or semicolon is critical.

How to Evaluate the Answers

The key word is "predict": You must predict the correct answer. This is done by determining what (if anything) is wrong with the underlined portion of the sentence. In the above example, the word "who" is incorrect. It should be "whom" (an explanation of "who/whom" is given in the practice exam).

You have now predicted that the word should be "whom." Look at the answer key and eliminate any answers without the word "whom." This narrows your answers down to D or E. Note how you have automatically increased your chances of getting the question right along with saving yourself much time.

Now, read the two possible answer choices. Note that D is identical to the original (that is, to the underlined portion of the sentence) with the exception of the word "whom." You have not changed anything; all you have done is corrected the error. Answer E, on the other hand, has corrected the error but changed the tense of the sentence. You should not change anything more than you absolutely have to. Therefore, D is the best choice.

Multiple "Correct" Answer Choices

Suppose you have a question like this:

<u>The man who is my mother's father</u> is a complete stranger to me; we have never met.

A. The man who is my mother's father
B. The father of my mother
C. My grandfather
D. My maternal grandfather
E. My grandfather (on my mother's side)

All of the answers are correct. That is, each answer is grammatically correct. All of the answers are logical (they all refer to the same person, my mother's father). How do you determine which answer is best? You choose the answer that is the most succinct, the most precise, without changing the meaning. Answer C may seem to be the best answer (it *is* the shortest); however, it is not precise. A person has two grandfathers, a father's father and a mother's father. Answer C does not tell which one is being discussed. Answer D is the best answer because it is concise as well as exact. It states the idea in just a few words.

NOTE: The original version, "The man who is my mother's father" is awkward and verbose. If the person is a father, he is certainly a man; therefore, it is unnecessary to say "The man." Your mother's father is your grandfather; it is better to say "maternal grandfather" than "the father of my mother." In brief, you may find you have more than one answer that is grammatically correct and logically correct. In such an instance, choose the *most concise and precise* answer.

The Best Approach

As soon as you see a question, take the following three step approach.

1. *Read the entire sentence carefully.* Try to understand what it is saying.

2. *Note exactly* how much of the sentence is underlined.

3. *Determine* whether there is an obvious error in the underlined portion, a grammar mistake that "jumps out" at you, or an awkward construction that could be better written.

Next, predict the correct answer with the following three steps.

1.   *Correct any grammatical errors.* For example, *lie* might be used when *lay* is required, or a plural verb might be used when a singular verb is required.

2.   *Reconstruct the sentence if it is written awkwardly.* In other words, if there is no one- or two-word error, but the whole sentence is awkward, redo it. Ask yourself how you would state it to make it logical and smooth. *Do not actually write the sentence down;* only "write" it in your mind.

3.   *Look for this answer in the answer key.* If you have corrected a one- or two-word grammatical error, look for the answer choices that have the correct word (such as "whom" instead of "who" in the example above). If you have rewritten the entire sentence, look for your new version among the answer choices.

Next, *check* the answer you have selected by the following three steps:

1.   *Make certain the answer fits into the original sentence and makes sense.* Often, people are trapped by an answer that is grammatically correct and looks good alone, but makes no sense when inserted into the original sentence.

2.   *Make certain your answer corrects any grammatical error or awkwardness found in the original sentence.* Be certain also that while you have corrected one error, you have not made another. Read the entire answer selection, not just the first few words.

3.   *Make certain that you have chosen the* best *answer*, the one that is the most concise and precise.

Traps to Avoid

In reading the *question* itself, there are three traps to avoid.

1.   *Do not read into the question more than is actually written there.* For example, a sentence may say, "John is not and never has a blonde;

he is a brunette." You may accidentally read, "is not and never has *been*" because that is what is correct and what you would usually see. Do not put in extra words; read the sentence *exactly* as written. Otherwise, you may find yourself thinking that there are a lot of sentences with no errors.

2. *Note exactly how much of the sentence is underlined.* Do not assume that a punctuation mark (such as a comma, semicolon, or colon) is underlined; check to be certain.

3. *Read the whole sentence, not just the underlined portion.* Often, there will be an error in the underlined portion only because of something found in the rest of the sentence. For example, a sentence may say, "Karen likes it, but I have never enjoyed Geometry and Algebra." Although there is nothing wrong per se with the word "it," it is incorrect here because it is referring to the words "Geometry" and "Algebra." The plural pronoun, them, must be used. If you just read the underlined portion, it would sound correct; you don't note an error until you read the rest of the sentence.

In reading the *answer choices*, there are three traps to avoid.

1. *Do not assume that just because you have corrected the obvious error the whole answer is grammatically correct.* In the first example given in this section, the *whom* was correct in answer E, but the rest of the sentence changed the tense and thus was incorrect. Read the entire answer choice.

2. *Do not correct an error and forget to reinsert the answer into the original sentence.* After you have corrected the error, reread the original sentence with your answer choice inserted. Many people skip this step, thinking they are saving time. They do save time, but lose points because their grammatically correct answer makes no sense in the sentence.

3. *Don't stop reading the answer choices when you feel you have the right answer.* This section is a test of good-better-best, not just of right or wrong. Just because you have a "correct" answer choice does not mean it is the best answer choice. Read all choices, then decide.

Time-saving Suggestions

1. *Predict an answer, then look for that answer in the answer key.* Predicting an answer will save you much time, as you will not have to anguish over two or more answers that all "seem correct." Usually your predicted answer is the best.

2. *Read from the bottom to the top.* Read answer choice E first, then D, C, and B. Do not read answer choice A. Since it is the same as the underlined portion of the sentence, you have already read it. You do not want to repeat yourself.

3. *Do not read any obviously incorrect answer choices.* If you have decided that "whom" must be used, not "who," do not take the time to read the answer choices beginning with "who." NOTE: Many people are insecure and read all the choices, "just to be sure." Such people do not finish this section. If you have completed the practice exam on this section and learned the rules given in the answer explanations, you should be sufficiently self-confident to be able to eliminate at least two or three answers on most questions.

Practice Exam: Sentence Correction

Please take the following practice exam on sentence correction. This practice exam consists of 15 questions with an answer key and explanatory answers following. Score yourself and remember: Incorrect answers cost you ¼ point each!

DIRECTIONS: In each of the following sentences, either all or part of the sentence is underlined. Below each question are five ways of stating the underlined portion; "A" is the same as the underlined portion in the question.

This section tests standard written English. Choose the answer that gives a grammatically correct sentence, is not ambiguous, and does not change the meaning of the original. Circle the letter before your answer.

1. Neither my girlfriends nor my boyfriend <u>is able to go shopping with me</u> this afternoon.

    A. is able to go shopping with me
    B. are able to go shopping with me
    C. is shopping with me
    D. are shopping with me
    E. shops with me

2. The news media <u>is undergoing an investigation by</u> the United States Congress this year.

    A. is undergoing an investigation by
    B. are undergoing an investigation by
    C. undergoes an investigation by
    D. undergo an investigation by
    E. could be undergoing an investigation by

3. Whenever <u>I tell my dog to go lay down</u>, he merely gives me a dirty look and continues chasing his tail.

    A. I tell my dog to go lay down,
    B. I tell my dog to lay down,
    C. I ask my dog to lay down,
    D. I tell my dog to go lie down,
    E. I tell my dog to go lie,

4. <u>Everyone is eager to get their hands on the author's newest book.</u>

    A. Everyone is eager to get their hands on the author's newest book.
    B. Every one is eager to get their hands on the author's newest book.
    C. Everyone are eager to get their hands on the author's newest book.
    D. Everyone are eager to get his hands on the author's newest book.

E. Everyone is eager to get his hands on the author's newest book.

5. No one is able to predict what the weather will be like for our picnic <u>this weekend, however, we are</u> betting that the sun will shine most of the day.

   A. this weekend, however, we are
   B. this weekend; however, we are
   C. this weekend; however; we are
   D. this weekend: however, we are
   E. this weekend; however: we are

6. <u>Grinning idiotically, the camera made Nellie look like a fool.</u>

   A. Grinning idiotically, the camera made Nellie look like a fool.
   B. Grinning idiotically, Nellie was made to look like a fool by the camera.
   C. Grinning idiotically, Nellie looked like a fool to the camera.
   D. Nellie, grinning idiotically, looking like a fool.
   E. Nellie looked like a fool, grinning idiotically.

7. Because Mother had been asking me to sweep the floor for a week, she had trouble believing me <u>when I told her that I had done it this morning.</u>

   A. when I told her that I had done it this morning.
   B. when I told her that I had done so this morning.
   C. when I told her that I did it this morning.
   D. when I told her this morning that I had done it.
   E. when I did it this morning.

8. The receptionist looked up politely when I asked for an appointment <u>and asked what it was in regards to.</u>

   A. and asked what it was in regards to.
   B. asked what it was in regards to.
   C. , asking what it was in regards to.
   D. and asked what it was in regard to.
   E. and asked what it is in regard to.

9. <u>Laughing like crazy men seem to be</u> a habit of my fraternity brothers.

    A. Laughing like crazy men seem to be
    B. Laughing like crazy men seems to be
    C. Laughing like crazy men are
    D. Laughing like crazy men is
    E. Laughing and being crazy men seems

10. <u>Few of the remaining students are actually studying;</u> most seem to be in a state of shock that the exam is today!

    A. Few of the remaining students are actually studying;
    B. Few of the remaining students is actually studying;
    C. Few of the remaining students are actually studying,
    D. Few of the remaining students is actually studying,
    E. Few actual studying students remain;

11. <u>Watching the rivers raise,</u> swelling their banks, we were awed by the majesty of Nature.

    A. Watching the rivers raise,
    B. We watched the rivers raise,
    C. We, watching the rivers raise,
    D. Watching the rivers rise,
    E. We watched the rivers rise,

12. <u>Harvey inferred from the look</u> on the woman's face that she was hoping he would ask her for a date that weekend.

    A. Harvey inferred from the look
    B. From the look, Harvey inferred
    C. Harvey implied from the look
    D. From the look, Harvey implied
    E. Harvey inferred the look

13. <u>The students try to always be on time,</u> but most of them seem to be unable to avoid being late at least once a week.

    A. The students try to always be on time,
    B. The students always are on time,

C. The students try to be on time always,
D. Always the students are trying to be on time,
E. The student tries to always be on time,

14. <u>I wonder who I should appoint to be</u> my successor; no one seems willing to work as hard at the job as I have done.

   A. I wonder who I should appoint to be
   B. I am wondering who I should be appointing to be
   C. I wondered who I should have appointed to be
   D. I wonder whom I should appoint to be
   E. I wonder whom I should have appointed to be

15. My mother warned us <u>that everyone should be on their best behavior</u> while the guest speaker was talking.

   A. that everyone should be on their best behavior
   B. that everyone should be on his best behavior
   C. that every one should be on their best behavior
   D. that every one should be on his best behavior
   E. that everyone should behave

ANSWER KEY

1. A	5. B	9. B	13. C
2. B	6. B	10. A	14. D
3. D	7. B	11. D	15. B
4. E	8. D	12. A	

Explanations

1. **(A)** With the "neither/nor" and "either/or" constructions, the number of the noun following the "nor" or the "or" determines the number of the verb. Here, the singular noun "boyfriend" follows the "nor"; therefore, the singular verb "is" is required. Answers C and E are grammatically correct but change the meaning of the sentence.

2. **(B)** "Media" is plural and requires a plural verb, "are." Answer E is grammatically correct but changes the meaning of the sentence.

3. **(D)** "Lie" is required because the dog is being told to recline. Answer E makes no sense when inserted into the sentence.

4. **(E)** "Everyone" is the subject and is singular; it requires a singular verb, "is" and a singular pronoun "his."

5. **(B)** When two separate sentences are joined by a conjunction (such as however), the proper form is semicolon, conjunction, comma, such as "; however,"

6. **(B)** This sentence begins with a subordinate clause, and erroneously states that the camera is doing the grinning. "Nellie" needs to follow the subordinate clause because she is doing the grinning. Answers C and E are grammatically correct, but change the meaning of the sentence. Answer D is a fragment, not a complete sentence.

7. **(B)** The pronoun "it" may only refer to a specific place or thing; "so" refers to actions (such as sweeping the floor). Only the correct answer has the "so"; you should not have taken the time to read the other answers at all, since they all had the incorrect word "it."

8. **(D)** The expression "in regards to" is incorrect. The proper form is "in regard to." Answer E is incorrect because of the improper tense of the verb ("is," rather than "was").

9. **(B)** A verb phrase functioning as a subject is always singular and requires a singular verb. Here, the subject is "laughing like crazy men." Answers D and E change the meaning of the sentence.

10. **(A)** The sentence is correct as written because "few" is plural and requires a plural verb, "are." The semicolon (;) is correct because it connects two separate sentences. The comma in answer C would make the sentence into a run-on.

11. **(D)** "Raise" requires an object (you raise something, such as raising your hand); "rise" requires no object (you don't rise something). In this instance, there is no object; the rivers

themselves are rising. "Rise" is correct. Answer E has rise, but would be incorrect when inserted into the original sentence.

12. **(A)** To infer is to conclude, to deduce, and is correctly used here. Harvey concluded that the woman wanted him to ask her out. To *imply* is to suggest. Perhaps the woman implied that Harvey ask her out; however, Harvey himself inferred that she wanted to be asked out. Answers B and E have the correct word, "infer," but would make no sense when reinserted into the sentence.

13. **(C)** The sentence has a split infinitive, which traditional grammarians consider to be improper usage. The infinitive is "to be," and is split by the adverb "always." You may avoid a split infinitive by putting the adverb elsewhere, usually right before the verb or at the end of the clause. In this instance, the correct answer moves "always" to the end of the clause. Answer D eliminates the split infinitive, but changes the meaning of the sentence unnecessarily.

14. **(D)** "Who" is subjective and is used as the subject of a sentence. "Whom" is objective and is used as the object of a verb or a preposition. In this case, "whom" is necessary because it is the object of the verb, "appoint." Answer E has the correct word "whom" but changes the meaning of the sentence.

15. **(B)** *Everyone* is singular and requires a singular verb and singular pronoun. This sentence must state that everyone should be on "his" or "her" or "his or her" best behavior. "Their" is incorrect because it is a plural pronoun. "Everyone" is correctly written as one word when used in the sense of "all the persons." Answer E changes the meaning of the sentence.

NUMBER RIGHT:____(Give yourself one point for each.)

NUMBER WRONG:____(Multiply by ¼ point each.)

FINAL SCORE:____(Subtract the second number from the first; you may have an answer with a fraction, such as 11¼.)

STUDY CALENDAR

10-HOUR STUDY SCHEDULE

	DAY 1	DAY 2	DAY 3	DAY 4	DAY 5
HOUR ONE	Suggested: Introduction Completed: TIME:	Suggested: Antonyms and Analogies Completed: TIME:	Suggested: Math Review Completed: TIME:	Suggested: Quantitative Comparisons Completed: TIME:	Suggested: Usage Completed: TIME:
HOUR TWO	Suggested: "The SAT" Completed: TIME:	Suggested: Sentence Completion and Reading Comprehension Completed: TIME:	Suggested: Math Review (continued) Completed: TIME:	Suggested: Problem Solving Completed: TIME:	Suggested: Sentence Correction Completed: TIME:

For In-Depth Preparation for the SAT*

PREPARATION FOR THE SAT—SCHOLASTIC APTITUDE TEST

by Edward J. Deptula—General Editor

The latest edition of Arco's acclaimed SAT test prep book offers expanded review of all subject areas tested on the SAT. Question-answering strategy is provided for all test areas and question types: mathematical abilities, verbal abilities (antonyms, verbal analogies, reading comprehension, and sentence completion), as well as for the Test of Standard Written English. The new sections covering test-wise principles will benefit all test-takers no matter how much time they have to prepare for their test.

Eight full-length practice examinations including a Diagnostic SAT and detailed answer explanations are provided.
Arco / 0-13-700865-1, paper

SUPERCOURSE FOR THE SAT

by Thomas H. Martinson

SuperCourse for the SAT is the dynamic professional coaching program recommended by educators and counselors everywhere! Its specially designed lesson-by-lesson format simulates the actual classroom experience of a top-quality coaching school. In addition, its colorful, eye-catching graphics aid comprehension and make learning easier.

The author, a professional SAT coach, offers hundreds of proven strategies specially developed by coaching schools. Easy-to-follow "walk-through" drills reveal the hidden pitfalls in each question type. Thousands of sample questions—with explanations—provide the most complete practice for the SAT now available in print.
Arco / 0-13-788506-7, paper

(see next page)

VERBAL WORKBOOK FOR THE SAT

by Walter James Miller, Elizabeth Morse-Cluley,
Gabriel P. Freedman and Margaret A. Haller

A complete self-teaching text and comprehensive review for the
Verbal and TSWE sections of the Scholastic Aptitude Test. Arco's
Verbal Workbook offers a graded and systematic plan for SAT
preparation.

Diagnostic tests with detailed solutions evaluate how much SAT
study is necessary. Worked-through sample problems increase
question-answering facility to give confidence for taking the actual
test. Drill questions graded from easy to difficult provide intensive
study and improve comprehension of each question type. Five
graded SAT verbal tests with self-progress charts will analyze overall SAT aptitude.

Arco
0-668-06135-9, paper

MATHEMATICS WORKBOOK FOR THE SAT

by Brigitte Saunders with David Frieder
and Mark Weinfeld

Combining authoritative instructional text and ample drill material for
the math areas covered on the SAT and other college entrance exams, this workbook is a necessary study aid for all college-bound
students.

For each math area there is a diagnostic exam to assess strengths
and weaknesses, practice questions, and a retest of the material.
Explanatory answers are given at the end of each chapter. Sample
SAT math tests are also provided.

Arco
0-668-06138-3, paper

(see next page)

VOCABULARY BUILDER FOR THE SAT

by Edward J. Deptula, Juliana Fazzone and Thomas H. Martinson

In its 20-lesson format, this book introduces 30 new words per lesson. Words are first presented in a reading passage, which is then followed by a vocabulary quiz consisting of a matching quiz and antonym and analogy questions. Reading passages are entertaining and stimulating. Answers to all quiz questions contain information on word meaning, word derivations, unusual words, and question structure. A final exam is included.

Arco / 0-668-06369-6, paper